# Longing for Africa

## Journeys Inspired by the Life of Jane Goodall

### Part One: Ethiopia

By
Annie Schrank

# Dedication

For Grover
It's a big, beautiful world, and love makes it even better.

*When I look back over my life it's almost as if there was a plan laid out for me—from the little girl who was so passionate about animals, who longed to go to Africa and whose family couldn't afford to put her through college. Everyone laughed at my dreams. I was supposed to be a secretary in Bournemouth.*

*People said, "Jane, forget about this nonsense with Africa. Dream about things you can achieve."*

Jane Goodall, Ph.D., DBE
Founder, the Jane Goodall Institute &
UN Messenger of Peace

# Contents

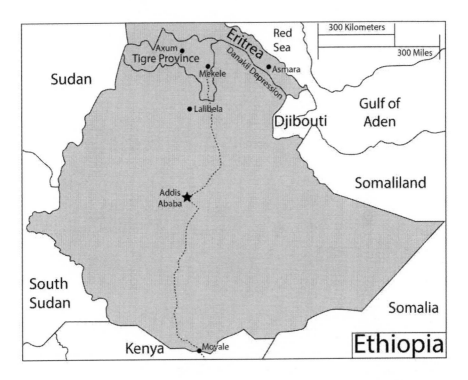

Photographs to accompany the book are available on the author's website:
www.annieschrank.com

# 1/ Arrival: Addis Ababa

The Ethiopian Airlines stewardess touched my shoulder. I awoke to a high-altitude African sunrise of red, orange, and fuchsia spread across the horizon. Our plane was about to land in Addis Ababa, the capital of Ethiopia, after sixteen hours in the air. My mouth was dry, my legs were cramped, and the large African man beside me had the most awful body odor. I struggled to sit upright and fastened my seatbelt. I pressed my forehead to the small window beside me and stared with wonder at the timeless tableau spread out below.

Africa.

I saw diminutive round huts topped with pointed thatched roofs in small clearings carved from the bush beside the airport runway. Lazy threads of smoke from cooking fires rose to meet the morning mist clinging to the ground. The roaring plane took one pass over the airport and scattered the goats and camels grazing on the tarmac. It banked and circled so close to the roofs that I could see women tending the fires, infants tied to their backs. Naked toddlers crawled and chickens pecked in the dirt.

Although the scene was entirely foreign to me, it felt familiar. I had kept what I called my Africa scrapbook from the time I could be trusted with a pair of scissors and a roll of tape, collecting photographs, articles, and anything about Africa I found. I'd been preparing for this moment since I was six years old.

I was twenty now and had grown up torn between two opposite fantasies. There was Cinderella in her pale blue ballgown and long white gloves, waltzing serenely in the arms of a handsome Prince Charming, secure in the knowledge that she had found true love, royal in-laws, and a castle home. And then there was Jane Goodall in her rumpled khakis from the pages of *National Geographic* and *Life* magazines—the heroine of my scrapbook.

She was my Jane, alone with her chimpanzees, her canvas safari tent in the Tanzanian rain forest, and, most of all, her courage. Her story captivated me; I followed her life avidly. I knew her favorite chimps—David Greybeard, Flo, and Flint—and swooned from the romance of it all when she fell in love with Hugo van Lawick, a photographer sent by *National Geographic*, whose presence in the rain forest she had initially resisted. Even Jane found her Prince Charming.

1

As I took in the scene below from the low-flying plane, the Jane in me was astonished by what I had set into motion in New York, but Cinderella was terrified.

When I walked down the rollaway metal staircase, blinking in the sun and groggy from sixteen hours of flying, even the air smelled like I thought it would. It's a smell I can still conjure up immediately, no matter where I am; a smell peculiar to Africa that is part spices, vegetables, and flowers, part animal and human waste, part sun-scorched earth.

I followed the other passengers across the tarmac to Customs and waited in line nervously for my turn, unable to read the signs—an indecipherable Ethiopian script of squiggles and dots. This was my first transatlantic flight with my first passport and visa. I cowered from the armed soldiers standing at attention wherever I looked.

A Customs official waved me forward. He studied my American passport and carefully read every word of the visa document.

"You are American. I do not see many American passports," he commented in heavily accented English. "What is the purpose of your visit? Business or pleasure, M'dam?"

"Business."

He looked at me with a bit more interest.

"What is the exact nature of your business, M'dam?"

"I'm here to set up a leather garment factory as a guest of Emperor Haile Selassie and the Governor of Tigre Province, Ras Mengesha."

Saying it aloud, standing on African soil, made it real.

Two days before, I had been living in a fifth-floor walk-up tenement apartment in Greenwich Village—a young fashion designer with my first actual design job. I created leather jeans, jackets, and vests, the latest in early '70s hippie/rock 'n' roll fashion. Think Sonny and Cher, Janis Joplin, the Eagles—fringe, conchos, embroidery, leather, and fur.

My boss had met the grandson-in-law of Emperor Haile Selassie and the governor of a northern mountainous province, Ras Mengesha. As seatmates in first class on a flight across the Atlantic, they came up with a business plan that could benefit them both, decades before global garment production.

Ethiopia had a small tannery that produced beautiful, soft cowhide, but, other than an Italian shoe company, there were no other outlets for the skins. My company could provide the expertise in design, patterns, production, and the final distribution of the finished garments to American department stores and boutiques. The partnership would provide a fashion product at a good price and offer steady jobs for Ras Mengesha's people. It was my first design job, and I knew very little about setting up a factory. But I was the only one from my company with the necessary knowledge who was willing to relocate to Africa. For me, it was my heart's greatest desire.

"How long will you be in Ethiopia?" the official continued his interrogation.

"Two years."

"Where are you going to live?"

"A town in the mountains in the north, Mekele."

"Yes, Mekele...That is very far away from Addis Ababa. I wish you success. I hope you will learn to love our country," he said, stamping my passport and visa with bureaucratic efficiency and dismissing me.

"Thank you, officer. I already do."

That was me in a nutshell, always needing to please, always wanting to be the good girl.

The luggage from the flight had been unloaded haphazardly in an open area next to Customs, guarded by more soldiers with machine guns slung across their chests, and I struggled through a sea of shoving, fellow passengers shouting in an indecipherable language, to reach the mountain of baggage that had been thrown one on top of the other. There were battered suitcases tied with rope or duct tape, crushed cardboard boxes, and string bags, oddly and solidly packed, some leaking. I was the only Caucasian in the group, the only female pushing her way to the front, and certainly the only traveler searching for three pieces of brand new, matching luggage, and a dog carrier.

I fought for my bags and let Daisy, my Beagle, out of her crate. I had packed a patchwork quilt from my childhood bed, but it was Daisy who, I knew, would provide the most comfort to me and my link to home. It may have been unwise to bring a domesticated pet dog to a continent of wild animals, but to me it was non-negotiable.

I poured some bottled water into my palms for Daisy and looked around. Most of the people in the terminal were tall, graceful, and long limbed with delicate, chiseled features and light skin the color of almond shells. They looked more Arab than African, refined and very beautiful. Most were dressed in white cotton—the men in long tunics and matching loose trousers, the women in white gauze dresses and necklaces of hammered silver and roughly-shaped amber beads.

Men and women alike wore long lengths of white chiffon, wrapped like shawls around them from head to hips. Pushing and jostling alongside the Ethiopians were Indians in vibrantly colored silk saris and an abundance of gold jewelry, or knee-length embroidered silk tunics and narrow pants. They stood out like tropical flowers in a sea of white.

Because there would be no one at the airport to meet me, I left the terminal to find a taxi. I struggled with Daisy, now on her leash, and the few bags I could handle by myself. I found a taxi waiting by the curb, dented and scraped, with bald, mismatched tires.

"Too good taxi, M'dam…the best," said the driver, a man as thin as a nail, of about thirty years of age, with a balding head to match his tires, wearing a much-laundered, short-sleeved, white shirt, dulled black cotton trousers, and open sandals made from recycled tires on his bare, callused feet. He opened the passenger-side door, scrambled over the front seat to the back, and opened the door for me from the inside.

"I am too happy to take you to any place in Addis. I know all hotels and streets," he said, his chest puffed up and out, nodding vigorously with a manic smile on his face.

I pulled a piece of paper from my shoulder bag. On it, I had the name and phone number of the American couple, my future co-workers, I would be meeting the next day, and the name of the hotel they had recommended for my first night.

"Do you know the Presidente Hotel?" I asked, showing the driver the paper.

"Oh, yes, M'dam. I know it too good. My name, it is Tedesu. I will take you there too quick." He forced open the trunk with a screwdriver and rushed to load in the first two suitcases, just in case I was planning to change my mind.

"Tedesu, I'm pleased to meet you. My name is Annie, and this is Daisy," I said.

"No, M'dam. Your name, it is M'dam."

"Can you please watch my dog while I go back inside for the rest of my luggage?" I naively held out Daisy's leash to him.

"The dog, M'dam?" He looked at Daisy suspiciously.

"Please, yes…my dog," I replied, worried he would expect Daisy to ride in the trunk. "Will it be all right if she sits in the back with me?"

Tedesu shrugged his narrow shoulders. Anything was okay with him, if it would result in a fare, a tip, and something for dinner.

I ran back into the terminal for another battle for my remaining bags, and, when I returned, Tedesu was sitting sideways on the back seat, the car door wide open, his feet resting on the sidewalk, and Daisy by his side.

"Sit, M'dam, and I will show you the too beautiful sights of the world-famous Addis Ababa."

I sat back to enjoy the "too beautiful sights," the non-functioning air-conditioning, and the feel of ripped, greasy upholstery held together with gray duct tape. My door window was frozen open, and my door handle was gone. Tedesu had used a wrench to open the door from the inside.

Driving through the streets of the capital, it all looked exactly as I had imagined it. The years I'd spent building my scrapbook made the reality of this African city feel more like a homecoming than a new experience. I stared out the open window at the crowded street markets jammed with colorful baskets of spices, fruits, and vegetables displayed on the ground.

Patient market women squatted in the dust behind each produce pile, shielding their eyes from the sun. The lucky ones sat beneath loose awnings of red, green, royal blue, and yellow cotton.

There were long-horned cattle, goats, donkeys with firewood stacked on their backs, and camels with precariously balanced burdens on their single humps and bells around their long necks, all herded through the city streets. They competed with the automobile traffic—the overloaded lorries and battered taxis, an ancient bus or two, and an occasional black Mercedes, as black and sleek as a jaguar.

The honking, the crowds and the pushing, the haze of heat and dust, the bleating of the goats and camels, the smells, and the press of regal-looking Ethiopians in white cotton and gauze with heavy, beaten, silver Coptic crosses and chunky amber on their chests simultaneously invaded my senses. The scene was madness—an exotic Manhattan with the streets filled with camels, goats, and cattle.

We made slow progress through the streets, allowing the animals the right of way or choosing side streets to avoid them. After one turn, we found ourselves stopped in the crosswalk, blocked from moving forward or backward by a mass of angry young men, most in threadbare Western-style clothing, marching and loudly chanting with their fists pumping in the air. They parted down the middle as they reached our taxi and flowed around us, slamming their open palms and fists against the taxi's roof and doors. Impassive soldiers fingered the AK47s slung diagonally across their chests, watching from the sidewalks.

Daisy barked furiously, ready to throw herself through the open window.

"What's happening?" I leaned forward, yelling to Tedesu to make myself heard over the shouted chants and holding Daisy back as best I could. "What is this? Please…tell me what's happening?"

"No good, M'dam," he said. "We shall stay calm, and they will pass this street."

"But what is it?" I asked again, panicked.

"The university students, they protest to the emperor. The classroom lectures, they are missing," he said. "This I know is a fact. I have one brother studying at university. His desire is for to be an electrical engineer. Three days ago, he marched with the students. He throw one rock to a soldier and they arrest him. Where the soldiers take him, we do not know. My mother, she is…" His English failed him. "I and my father, we go at night to the jails. The soldiers tell to us, my brother's name is not on the list. He is missing three days now."

Tedesu's expression never changed as he spoke. He had told me the truth and was no longer playing the role of a taxi driver saying what he needed to say to earn a fare, a huckster hidden behind a nodding head, a

5

grin, and popping eyes. As he told me the story of his brother, there was no anger, no sadness; just the flat acceptance of a poor man's fate.

"I'm so sorry," I told him, shrinking back into my seat and cringing as if I'd been slammed between the eyes.

I didn't know it yet, but this was the beginning of the protests against Emperor Haile Selassie's government that would grow in size and power during the next year and, at the apex of its ferocity, include the emperor's own army. A Communist-backed military coup would bring to an end the longest continuous monarchy in world history, one that dated back to King Solomon and the Queen of Sheba. It would affect everyone in this country. It would rip people away from their loved ones, hurling the luckiest among them, including myself, across oceans.

Tedesu and his taxi were not the target of the protestors' rage, just an obstacle in the road. But I sat in the back seat, holding my breath and the back of Tedesu's seat, as the crowd of young men surged around and past us. With every fist slammed against the taxi roof, Daisy exploded into a new paroxysm of barking. And then the protestors were gone, and we were able to drive on, Tedesu cautiously peering around corners first, taking side streets the rest of the way. I sat deep in my seat, twisting sections of my long hair between my thumb and index finger, a nervous habit I had used to calm myself since I was a little girl.

"Here we are, M'dam." Tedesu braked in front of a building on a crowded main street that looked like an American two-story supermarket from the front. "You are here at the Presidente Hotel. I am too sorry about the danger problem in the street."

"No, Tedesu," I said. "No, I'm so sorry for you and your family. I hope you find your brother soon, and you can bring him home."

I had to pull at Daisy's leash a few times to get her to reluctantly jump from the taxi to the sidewalk. She was frightened by the onslaught of new aromas at the curb and refused to jump down. She'd never smelled camel or goat dung and urine before.

"Thank you, M'dam. You go in, and I bring too many luggages. You take M'dam Daisy."

The Presidente Hotel was considered a mid-priced hotel in Addis Ababa. The lobby was shadowed, even with the bright morning sun streaming through the plate glass. It was shabby, with a single Formica counter for the front desk, scuffed linoleum squares, and dusty armchairs so worn that their color had no name. This was not promising, but it was where I'd been asked to stay for the night, and where my family in New York could reach me.

If I'd been older and more confident, I would have walked right back out to the street, hailed the first taxi I saw, and asked to be taken to the best hotel in the city. But the lobby was reassuringly busy with Africans and

Indians and a few white faces rushing from the single elevator to and from the dining room and the double plate-glass front doors. I was famished and could smell toasted bread and butter above the underlying aroma of dust and mold. The clerk who welcomed me in English took a look at Daisy and asked me, as if my answer made no difference to him, whether my companion in the room was "this dog."

I had requested a single room, expecting at least an American double, but my room really did come with a single bed. Everything in it was some shade of gray—dingy sheets, a rough blanket tucked in all the way around the bare bed frame, a dusty and stained carpet and drapes, a grimy, imitation wood dresser and nightstand with the veneer peeling away in spots, and not a single print on the wall. It felt more like a prison cell than a hotel room.

I paused in the doorway, but again made the decision to stay, concerned that Daisy would use the rug as a toilet, and, in a better hotel, that might become a problem. At least at the Presidente, one more stain would go unnoticed. But I had to get outside into the sunlight before I'd give in to my fears.

After changing money at the front desk, Daisy and I took a walk. The sun was already a shocking presence, pure and relentless, but we were twenty-five hundred feet above sea level, and the temperature was that of summer in New Hampshire. The insides of shops we passed were as dim as the Presidente's lobby. Our street had tea and coffee shops every few feet, Ethiopian restaurants, men's and women's clothing stores with Western-influenced garments on bruised Caucasian mannequins, and a beauty parlor with posters of fanciful, braided, cornrow styles—how most of the women wore their hair—against hot pink and turquoise backgrounds.

We followed some music until we found the source, a record store playing Ethiopian brass band marching music with a definite African beat that was unlike anything I'd ever heard before and irresistible. Ethiopians and Indians walked rapidly past us, and, occasionally, their eyes would slide from me to Daisy and back again, a curiosity that interested them for only a moment.

We turned onto a side street and I realized, too late, I'd made a mistake. We were swarmed by a gang of boys and girls who followed us, begging for change and calling me Mama, or silently moving their hands to their mouths, miming hunger with as little physical effort as possible. One had a deformed, curved spine and a caved-in rib cage that brought his face close to his waist. A few were missing a limb or an eye, and one had his paralyzed legs strapped across his bent knees to a piece of plywood on four roller skate wheels. His hands had taken the place of his feet, and were callused and splayed.

All were filthy, barefoot, and covered in pieces of rags. When I had given away all my Ethiopian coins, they grew insistent, circling us, pointing at Daisy and laughing. Daisy growled, but stayed close to my side, knowing the threat was too real for her to bluster her way through. Two passing men in sparkling white Ethiopian suits, wrapped in white shawls over their white tunics, took pity on me, not on the children, and beat them with rolled-up newspapers, yelling curses at them until they ran away.

The men pointed back to the main street and made sure I headed in that direction. Daisy and I sprinted back to the Presidente Hotel and up in the elevator. I gave in to my fear and my serious jet lag, collapsed on top of the scratchy blanket, and fell into an anxious sleep, unable to keep the disturbing images of the street children from my dreams.

I awoke hours later to a dark room, headachy and hungry. Daisy had to be starving as well. We'd traveled from New York with only kibble and dog biscuits for her. I walked her out to the curb to relieve herself, where her smells mingled with those of the cattle, goats, and camels. Then we returned to the hotel lobby and the cavernous, almost empty dining room. A headwaiter, dressed in a tuxedo that had been cleaned both too much and not enough, stood at attention by the entrance.

"I would like dinner, but may I bring my dog into the dining room?"

"Of course, M'dam. That will not be a problem at the Presidente." He gave a short, stiff bow, an unreadable expression on his face, and led us to a table set for four. Daisy, a year-old brown and white under-sized Beagle with short, stubby legs, and with long ears swinging, strutted across the floor on her leash to our table like a princess.

The waiter held out a chair first for Daisy, who jumped right up onto the seat, and then for me. He handed me a menu in English. Another expressionless and tuxedoed waiter brought two glasses to the table. Daisy normally ate from a bowl on the floor, but she seemed to understand there were now new rules. She took her place at the table as if she'd been doing it all her life.

"Would M'dam like still or fizzy water?" he asked.

Still or fizzy water? Caught off guard, I had no idea what he was asking me. In America in those days, water came from a faucet. I thought about it for a moment and realized "fizzy" water had to be seltzer water; that I knew. My grandmother had made chocolate sodas for us with Hershey's syrup, milk, and seltzer water.

"Still, please." Daisy, I knew, would not be too happy with seltzer.

The waiter warned me that traditional Ethiopian food was too spicy for most European palates, so I thought it wise to order conservatively. I had plenty of time ahead of me to try Ethiopian cuisine, so I ordered spaghetti and meatballs and didn't ask what kind of "meat" was in the meatballs. It was delicious, surprisingly delicious.

I had read everything I could about Ethiopia before I left the States, and knew that Italy had invaded the country twice and tried to annex Ethiopia for itself during World War II. They had been repelled both times, but had left behind a legacy of Italian customs, architecture, and, happily, Italian cuisine.

Daisy ate her steak dinner from a chair pulled up close to mine. She was well behaved and thrilled with the unimaginable quality and quantity of the beef on her plate. She didn't bark and didn't jump down to relieve herself by the table leg. After a few stares by the handful of diners spread out in the enormous room as we were being seated, no one even bothered to look at us.

Later, I lay wide awake for a long time, thinking about Tedesu and his lost brother, and about the beggar children, also lost, tossed away like trash into the streets. I wondered if they'd had anything to eat for dinner. Were they asleep in the alleys? Did they dream of their mothers, or only of a plate of food? Daisy slept, sated and snoring gently on the pillow, curled above my head.

I woke at midnight with a bad case of jet lag and stayed awake until morning, thinking about the stained porcelain in the bathroom, the dirty rug, how many people had slept beneath the same blanket. I watched the wind-up alarm clock on the nightstand and craved scrambled eggs and toast.

I thought about my Africa scrapbook to keep my spirits up. Other girls kept those pastel-colored plastic diaries with the locks that kept nobody out. I tore apart old *National Geographic* magazines and taped down photographs of Masai warriors with their spears, loping giraffes, rare white rhinos, spotted cheetahs in flight, snakes fifteen feet long and as thick as a man's thigh, Dr. Leakey and his discovery of the earliest known human remains at Olduvai Gorge. And always, always, the chimpanzees.

While other girls adored the Partridge Family, I idolized Jane Goodall. I devoured everything I read or saw about her. I wanted to *be* her— to live alone in the rain forest in a tent in Tanzania, to spend my days in the company of chimps, and to fall in love with a man like Baron Hugo Von Lawick. Along with the story of Cinderella and Prince Charming, this was my girlhood romantic fantasy—Jane and Hugo, seeking shelter from the rain in a tent, dressed in wrinkled khaki.

I worked on my scrapbook every chance I could, and, when I closed my eyes, I could see each photograph in its correct order. Every time I flipped the pages of my treasured scrapbook, like an incantation, I sensed I was bringing Africa closer to me.

I was proud of myself, the girl who had grabbed this opportunity. I belonged here—I knew it—and I embraced Africa immediately and completely. On my first day in Ethiopia, I had been plunged into the life of an African city—exuberant music and colors, begging children, disappearing brothers, violence, AK47s, the feat of daily survival, an ocean of sorrow.

As I waited for morning in that dark hotel room, the sheltered, privileged life I'd led in the New York suburbs began to crack. I may have come to Africa in the footsteps of Jane Goodall, to do some good, to make a small change, but it was *Africa* that would change *me*. What I learned during the next year—how precious are our relationships with each other, how miraculous is the earth and its creatures—I've carried with me ever since.

## 2/ To Mekele: Mekele, Ethiopia

In the dark, I sat upright on the bed, not knowing where I was at first, and experiencing halfway-around-the-world jet lag for the first time. As soon as it was civilly possible, I called the young couple who would be my partners in the new factory. I'd already been told that Dean was a former American Peace Corps volunteer who had stayed on for our project, and his wife, Gemma, was a former British Peace Corp volunteer. They would be the eyes and ears of Ras Mengesha and the royal family, in charge of the money and the factory setup, and I would be responsible for the training and the product. I felt reassured when I heard their excited voices through the static and dead spots on the phone line. They invited me to lunch, and I breathed a little easier.

"I've brought my Beagle, Daisy, with me," I reluctantly let Dean know.

"Oh..." Dean said, nonplussed. "I guess that'll be fine. We love dogs...we do. Bring her to the house with you."

Dean said he would pick me up at noon, and we'd fly to Mekele together later in the afternoon. This was a surprise, but I was relieved and grateful not to spend another night at the Presidente.

We went in for breakfast, and, again, the maître d', inscrutable in his threadbare tuxedo, showed us to a table and pulled out a chair for Daisy. Without any coaxing from me, she jumped up, waited patiently while I ordered, and ate eggs and bits of toast from my hand. Her eyes locked onto the food, and she made happy little groans of pleasure between bites.

Back upstairs, I repacked, looked around the room for the last time with relief, and closed the door. I didn't want to spend another minute in that room. I staggered down the stairs to the lobby with my luggage.

To kill time, we walked up and down the main street, like we'd done the day before. The same African brass band marching music pulsated from the record store, and the country market women were back in their place on the sidewalks, sitting on their haunches before their new piles of fruits and vegetables. White-clad businessmen walked briskly in and out of the coffee shops, two by two, shoulders touching, with arms around each other's waists or even holding hands.

The goats bore their own weight in precariously balanced firewood, charcoal, coffee, or grain in canvas sacks, and stopped traffic as they were herded through the center of the road. A heavily-loaded camel decided not to take another step further and went down on its front knees right in front of me. Its owner cursed and beat it viciously again and again with a switch, but it moaned and refused to budge.

I couldn't bear to watch any longer and turned away from the cruelty, the callousness. I was reminded of the street children from the day before. Even in my sleep, they had been with me, the saddest thing I had ever witnessed in my sheltered, privileged American life. Bread, I decided. Then I'd find them and feed them.

I found a bakery by following the aromas of just-baked bread, yeast, and burned sugar, and stopped there to fill four white paper bags with rolls. When I paid at the counter, the shop owner spoke to me in English.

"You buy too many breads this morning, M'dam," he said.

"Yes, they're for the children, the ones near here who beg in the street."

"That is not a good idea, M'dam." He shook his index finger in warning. "You must have caution. They are thieves…bad children."

"I will take care," I said, "But can you translate a few English words into Amharic for me?"

"Yes, M'dam, most certainly."

As he spoke the Amharic words, he wrote their English approximation in pencil on another white paper bag.

"Bread."

"DaBo."

"Eat."

"BeLa."

"For you."

"EeNaNeTe."

"Share."

"FaNeTa."

"Thank you."

"TeNaStaLing."

Arms full, I looked for the side street where we'd seen the children the day before. I recognized the corner, and we turned in. Halfway up the block, I saw the boy strapped onto his plywood square. He pushed himself toward us, using his splayed hands and muscled arms to propel himself, faster than the other children. They appeared from doorways and alleys like stray dogs, running and crowding around us in seconds. Daisy stood by my side, shivering helplessly.

A little girl of perhaps nine pushed ahead of the others, covered from head to toe in dust, mimicking the sign for food. Her hair was unkempt, springing out from her head in dusty, matted tufts. The color was the gray of a discarded mop. Her feet were bare, with deep cracks along her dirty heels and soles. She wore a colorless, poncho-type garment that reached to her knees, a discarded grain sack or a rag. It, too, was covered in dust and grime. The look on her face was first cunning and desperate, but, when she looked directly at me, I could tell she remembered me from the day before, and something softened behind her eyes. She let her hands drop to her sides with fatigue. I handed her one of the baker's bags. She grabbed for it with panicky swiftness, but I held onto her arm before she could flee.

"For you...EeNaNeTe," I said. My first Amharic words. "Eat...Share."

I handed one to the boy on the wheeled platform.

"For you...Eat...Share."

I gave the third one to the boy with the curved spine and caved-in chest.

"For you...Eat...Share."

And the last one went to the youngest child, a boy who looked four or five, but may have been eight or nine.

"For you...Eat...Share," I told him, but I kept him by me, a hand on his shoulder, to protect him from an onslaught from the older children.

When they finished distributing the rolls between them and began to pull at my skirt and beg me for change, I turned away from them, chastened. I had fed my dog two meals from a table in a hotel dining room, ordering for her off a heavy printed menu the size of a magazine, while, three blocks away, children who had been tossed away like trash had spent the night in doorways and alleys, unprotected, unloved, hungry, and cold.

*****

Dean came for us in his car at exactly noon, and Daisy and I were waiting for him with my luggage in the lobby. He was handsomer than I expected—model handsome, tall and solid, with light brown hair, fair skin, a strong jaw and cheekbones. With his good health, good looks, and confident stride, he could only have been an American. We had a shy moment when we greeted each other, but, by the time we had loaded the car and settled in for the ride across the city, I knew we'd be friends.

He told me about his new wife, Gemma. They had met in Ethiopia, fallen in love, and married quickly in Addis only two months before, without their families. As he spoke of her, he seemed dazzled by their love for each other and their amazing luck. *How romantic*, I thought. It was what I wanted and fantasized about—to fall in love, like Jane and Hugo, like Gemma and Dean, in Africa.

"Addis traffic," Dean said, making a joke, nodding at the goats being herded by a tiny goatherd through an intersection as we waited.

"I took a taxi from the airport into town yesterday, and we got trapped by a student protest," I told him. "The driver told me his brother had been arrested and taken away. He's missing."

"I know," Dean said. "There's something serious happening in Addis." He honked at a goat that had suddenly bolted sideways in front of his car. "Lately it seems there's been a demonstration in the streets outside the emperor's palace every day, and they're getting more and more violent. University students and even professors, some junior army officers...they're chanting and throwing bottles and rocks. The students are angry that their classes have been cut, that the government is limiting the curriculum. The officers are protesting the lack of food for the soldiers. For the most part, the police just stand by and watch. Then something will set them off, and they will beat some of the young men badly, dump them in open trucks, and take them away."

"How awful," I said "What d'you think happens to them?"

"I can't be certain...beaten, for sure...tortured or killed, perhaps. Most never get returned to their families, like your taxi driver's brother. One of our Peace Corps employees disappeared almost a week ago—a nice guy, a husband and a father, not a troublemaker, someone we all liked a lot. We're doing everything we can to help his family."

"In what way?" I asked.

"We're making the rounds of the hospitals and prisons. We've sent his paycheck to his wife, collected cash for her. We're making calls to anyone we can think of who might know something. We've called the American consulate for help."

"And?"

"Nothing. Absolutely nothing," Dean admitted. "My gut tells me he's gone. They say the emperor's been shocked by the rebellion. Nothing like this has ever happened here before. He's promised the people he'll make changes, but, so far, nothing. And there's a rumor that he's turning the throne over to his son, but I don't know if that will make a difference. Haile Selassie's family has ruled Ethiopia for four hundred years. He can trace his family even further back to King Solomon. Imagine that."

"Yes...imagine that," I said. "But what has his family done for their people in the last four hundred years?"

"Nothing," Dean admitted. "Ethiopia is one of the poorest, most backward countries in the world."

The outskirts of Addis Ababa were like the outskirts of big cities everywhere—empty streets, trees, flowering gardens, quiet except for the sound of birdsong on that sunny, temperate afternoon. There were differences here in Addis—the streets were packed dirt, and the homes and gardens were hidden from view behind high, cinder-block-gated fences. The tops of compound walls were embedded with shards of colored, broken glass bottles, pointing wickedly straight up as a deterrent to thieves.

Dean gave two sharp blasts on his horn, and an *askiri* (private guard) opened the gates from inside. The lawn within was a brilliant green, with every blade of grass standing at attention, and a luscious flower garden was in riotous, full bloom. The house was a gray stone bungalow with white-painted trim, a screened side porch, and a front portico of climbing purple bougainvillea.

"Don't be too impressed," Dean said. "It's rented."

But I *was* impressed. Every young adult I knew lived like me in a college dorm or a walk-up apartment in Greenwich Village.

"There's Gemma," Dean smiled, pointing to where his wife was waiting by the front door, waving to us. Daisy ran right to her when I opened the car door, and Gemma bent down and took her into her arms.

Gemma was a perfect match for Dean's preppy good looks and that gracious home. She was a glamorous, tall blonde, an obviously upper-class girl from the Lake District in England. She was dressed like a modern British princess in a forest green plaid miniskirt with a matching twinset and pearls, while every other girl at that time wore hippie, peasant blouses, and embroidered denim. She tossed her gleaming, long hair away from her forehead with a flick of her hand again and again; a studied movement, but she struck me as warm and friendly. She welcomed me with sincere good manners.

"I'm so sorry we weren't able to meet you at the airport yesterday," she said. Daisy was still in her arms, squirming with joy and licking her cheeks and neck. "We didn't know exactly when you'd be arriving, and we only got back into town ourselves yesterday. Lunch is ready. Come inside to the table. Oh, Dean, darling! I love this dog!"

The dining room had a large picture window that looked over an overgrown, jumbled flower garden with mountains beyond. The walls were lined with white-painted bookshelves, crammed every which way with books and knick-knacks.

Lunch was a roasted chicken, small potatoes, and salad. Gemma was just learning to cook, and, even with a helper in the kitchen banging pots and pans, she had a long way to go; dry chicken and burned potato skins.

In her plummy, royal accent, Gemma began or ended every sentence with "Dean, darling," an exotic expression of endearment I had never heard before outside of a movie theater. The three of us liked each other right away, and I relaxed into the friendly conversation and the untidy house—piles of books and magazines lying around, throw rugs askew, clothing tossed over every piece of furniture. Daisy, too, was happy, and, although relegated to the kitchen during lunch, she was content with a meaty bone wider than she was.

They told me about another political situation in Eritrea Province that would, no doubt, affect us in Mekele. They were fighting for independence from Ethiopia in what would be, after another decade of violent warfare, a successful struggle to become the new nation of Eritrea. We didn't know that then—all we knew was that we would be living beside a province embroiled in a civil war with Communist-funded and -trained freedom fighters, rifles, hostages, and roadblocks on the one paved road through our province and the entire country.

If we wanted to drive the main road between Mekele and the Italian cities of Asmara or Masawa while we were living there, we would need written permission signed by Ras Mengesha to present to the *shiftas* (the rebels/freedom fighters/thieves/thugs) patrolling the temporary roadblocks through the countryside. *Why,* I thought, *if the shiftas were rebelling against the government and the emperor, would they honor travel papers signed by a member of the royal family?*

"Innocent people, people like us, have been murdered by the *shiftas*," Dean said.

No one had mentioned any of this to me in New York, but here we were. I'm sure Ras Mengesha hadn't revealed this detail to my boss as they drank their way across the Atlantic. I just wouldn't write about any of it in my letters home.

"And with the protests here in the city…it's been frightening," Gemma continued. "First it was just the students and teachers demonstrating against the control the emperor has over their studies, but, for the last few days, junior army officers have joined them, demanding back pay, food, and water for their troops."

"The word is that they haven't been paid in months, maybe even years," Dean added.

"It looks like Haile Selassie's got problems," I frowned. "I almost feel sorry for him. For four hundred years his family got to do whatever they wanted, and now it looks like it's imploding around him."

"You can't count him out yet," Dean said. "He's a tough old hyena, and his army is as ruthless as he is."

That was a prophetic remark. It would be his hand-chosen army officers that would bring Haile Selassie down within the year and murder him while he was under house arrest shortly after.

"Dean, darling, I'm glad we're moving to Mekele," Gemma smiled at him. "The demonstrations will never reach the north. While we're there, we won't have to find a new route home every night or worry about our friends."

She seemed to forget about the civil war and the armed *shiftas* manning roadblocks in our backyard.

After lunch, the couple came by who would be renting Dean and Gemma's home, furniture, household help, books, and whatever was left in the fridge. Gemma excused herself to show them the peculiarities of the house, and Dean brought their luggage—a small mountain of it—out to the driveway. He looked at it forlornly, loaded in what he could fit with mine, and yelled to Gemma that he was leaving to make the first of three trips to the private airfield.

I waited in the living room and entertained myself with semi-recent issues of British *Vogue*. Feeling like I was relaxing in a home in the English countryside instead of Africa, I thought that, if Mekele was like this, I would be very comfortable in Ethiopia. It was so easy to retreat to what I had come from.

We left their home an hour later as if we would be gone for two hours instead of two years—open books and magazines, half-filled coffee cups on the dining table, a towel on the floor in the bathroom.

Dean had hired a small plane and a pilot to fly us to Mekele. It was a two-hour plane ride, four hundred-odd miles to the north and five thousand feet above Addis. The pilot spent a half hour rearranging our luggage in the tail of the plane before he assigned us our seats based on our weights. He handed us airsickness bags before we took off. We'd be flying over mountains with steep drop-offs that created lots of unstable air, he explained. It was best to be prepared.

And we were off. The mountains to the north of Addis were an isolated place, and they grew taller and more inaccessible the further north we flew. It was an unforgiving landscape with little water. Everything below us was some shade of beige—tan, mushroom, taupe, wheat, sand, fawn, coffee, cream, burlap, amber, dried mud. There was no green patchwork of farms and pastures, no rolling hills, no trees; just jagged, sandy mountains shaded on one side and bathed in bright sunlight on the other, with ravines lost in the deepest shadows.

This was not the Africa I imagined—not Jane Goodall's Tanzanian rainforest, nor the Kenyan savannas from my scrapbook where lions, elephants, and zebras wandered. From the air, it seemed that nothing below me moved. There were only the bare, looming, and secretive mountains, the empty sky, and, above it all, the insistent, searing sun. I rested my forehead against the windowpane and watched apprehensively the emptiness beneath us.

*How do people survive in this environment? How will we?*

"It's so desolate," I yelled above the engines, feeling pretty desolate myself.

"Ethiopia's in the middle of a famine right now," Dean shouted back. "Every ten years or so, a drought, followed by a famine, comes from the Sahara to the Horn of Africa. Tigre Province has been hit the hardest this time. A hundred thousand people have already died."

"There's a refugee camp outside of Mekele," Gemma yelled over her shoulder. "Perhaps we might want to help. A Bulgarian doctor and his wife run it. They're trying to make a go of it, but the government has been

**17**

keeping the famine a secret from the world. The emperor doesn't want to admit he can't take care of his people, so almost no relief supplies are coming into the country."

"What does arrive is stolen by officials and guards, right at the airport, or hijacked at *shifta* roadblocks," Dean added from the front seat. "I don't know how Dr. Horst's team keeps going with no food, no medicine, and no help. They'll be grateful for whatever time we can give them."

Gemma shook her head. "Wait and see, Annie. You're going to meet some incredible people."

I was getting more and more anxious the farther away from Addis we flew. Trying to get to the uncomfortable, anxious feeling in my stomach, thinking it through for a few minutes as the mountains grew higher and more inaccessible, I finally realized why. Except for my time away at college, I'd never lived more than walking distance from the Atlantic Ocean. I'd smelled the sea salt in the air my entire life.

I'd grown up under a New York bridge, a few blocks from Little Neck Bay and the Long Island Sound, and had sailed and water-skied with my family during the humid New York summers for most of my childhood. Even the West Village in Manhattan was only blocks from the Hudson River. The ocean meant freedom and escape to me, and I'd known nothing else. Now I'd be land-locked, seven thousand feet above the Indian Ocean, and surrounded by mountains even higher than that. It felt ominous, and the reality of my new life in Ethiopia clobbered me as if I'd been hit in the chest with a rock—a physical response.

Right then, the plane dropped abruptly. I grabbed for an airsickness bag, and Gemma and Dean politely looked away.

*****

"There's Mekele, to your left," the pilot said, yelling over his right shoulder. "We'll be on the ground in ten minutes."

Our new home lay in a deeply shadowed, bowl-shaped valley with high mountains encircling it. A half dozen unpaved streets with wood plank sidewalks, lined with mud-walled, single-story square shops formed the town center at the bottom of the basin. Narrow dirt roads and even narrower footpaths snaked up from all sides and into the mountains. Simple cinder-block homes—like Monopoly homes—had been built along these smaller roads. The roofs over those homes and the shops, a patchwork of corrugated tin, flashed in the sun.

Higher into the hills, the same round huts, with the pointed thatch roofs I'd seen alongside the tarmac at the Addis airport, lined the footpaths that disappeared into the mountain bluffs and cliffs. Some were built close together, enclosing small corrals for goats and camels, forming a compound. As we approached for the landing, I finally spotted a few small vegetable plots tucked between houses and huts, and an occasional shade tree. This was Mekele, the capital of Tigre Province.

At the very top of the tallest mountain surrounding Mekele stood a small, gray stone castle, three stories high, with crenellated rooflines and a tower at each of its four corners. It commanded a three-hundred-and-sixty-degree defensive view of the entire basin.

"That's the only hotel in town," Dean said over the whine of the engine, pointing to the looming, stone-bricked, fairytale structure. "We'll stay there tonight, have a nice dinner, and look for homes for ourselves tomorrow."

"It looks like something from the Middle Ages," I exclaimed.

"You're not that far off—only a thousand years or so. It's about five hundred years old. It was a real fort once, with this great vantage point overlooking the other mountains, but it's been turned into a hotel—not a great one, but then, not many tourists come to Mekele or Ethiopia for that matter. This is a pretty interesting part of the world. It's got some of the earliest known Christian churches carved out of the mountains, not far from here, but most of the tourists who visit Africa are interested in seeing wildlife. If they want to see churches, they go to Europe."

*I will really try to love this remote and lonely place*, I thought, as we landed flawlessly at an airfield carved between two mountains. *I will really try.*

# 3/ The *Tukol*: Mekele, Ethiopia

A Peace Corps acquaintance of Dean's met us with a battered, gray Land Rover. "This is all yours," he said to Dean, gesturing to the truck. "It's a present from Ras Mengesha and the good people of the United States of America. We're leaving here tomorrow. And Lela is waiting for you at the hotel. She had the kitchen make a huge pan of lasagna for you all. You're the only guests tonight."

Our drive to the hotel took us through the main street of Mekele, where I saw the shops and sidewalks that had seemed deserted from the air. It was a mountain version of Addis Ababa city life—the weary, enduring market women, still sitting on their heels in the late afternoon sun, hoping to sell the remaining produce in their baskets, the barber, the sandal maker, the tailor shop, the butcher, all servicing their last customers of the day in the open air.

Their shops were built from mud and straw, with one open wall—the size of a prison cell without bars, without windows. Razor-thin men and women wrapped in threadbare white shawls—a stained and discolored white, as if the color white had grown weary—walked along the wooden plank sidewalks, some carrying their bundles on their heads, some with babies on their backs or hips. Camels and goats herded by young boys commanded the right of way in the road. Ours was the only automobile in sight.

"The main shopping street," Dean said, waving his left arm out of the open window toward the scene.

*Now, this is Africa*, I thought, cheering up a bit. I imagined myself shopping with a handmade straw shopping basket, choosing an onion from one woman, adding fresh eggs from another, watching a third woman wrap a pinch of peppercorns in a twist of newspaper.

It took three or four minutes to cross the town and continue up the road leading to the fort we'd seen from the air. It was an imposing fortress, with walls and ramparts built entirely of stone blocks. Five hundred years ago, someone had chiseled those blocks out of a mountainside by hand.

A long, steep flight of stairs led to the front entrance, a pair of massive wooden doors set on enormous forged metal hinges. Wide terraces with waist-high, stone balustrades, empty and devoid of any potted greenery, bordered both sides of the castle. A solidly built, middle-aged Indian woman with long, gleaming black hair parted in the center, wearing a brilliant, fuchsia silk sari, waited for us at the top of the steps.

"Welcome to Mekele, Dean," she said in heavily accented English and a feminine musical lilt I found enthralling. "We've been expecting you all afternoon, and we saw the plane arrive just now. We're so happy you've come."

Dean presented Gemma.

"How beautiful you are," Lela said to her, taking both Gemma's hands in hers.

And he introduced me.

"How darling...an American hippie," she said, cryptically, taking in my scruffy sandals and bare toes, my long peasant skirt, my Mexican embroidered peasant blouse. "Welcome, my dear. Come inside. I hope we shall be good friends. I am Lela. Come to the dining room. I have tea ready for you," she smiled, guiding us inside. She looked at Daisy with surprise. "Let us take your dog to the back. The kitchen boys will take good care of her. They'll feed and entertain her for the night."

She spoke orders in a rapid, musical stream of Amharic, and her staff jumped to do her bidding. Daisy disappeared with one of them. Lela was used to being obeyed, and I kept any reservations I had to this plan to myself.

The walls of the empty dining room were golden, filled with late afternoon sunlight. The tables and chairs were modern, Swedish in style, light wood, draped with spotless, pressed white table cloths. Young waiters with long, white half-aprons tied around their waists bustled around us as we took tea with Lela and her husband, Rakesh, a quiet, elderly man who left the conversation and the hotel operations to his wife.

The hotel sparkled and smelled of lemon and furniture oil. She had trained her "boys" well. Her waiters watched her with complete concentration. A lift of her eyebrow or a tap of her painted fingernail on the white tablecloth was interpreted immediately into an unspoken but understood action.

"Why do you love this country so much?" I asked Gemma, Lela, and Dean as an anxious waiter poured chai tea.

Gemma answered immediately. "I know why I love it. Ethiopia is a country and culture that's been scrubbed by the sun to its most basic elements. There's nothing simpler than mountains and sky. No trees, no rainforest, no beaches, nothing soft—just like the fierceness and courage of the people."

"Ethiopia is full of contrasts," Lela added. "The white clothing against the dark skin and amber necklaces, the gold ornaments against the jewel-colored velvets and satins of the church, and the black mountains against the sunrise and the sunset..." Her voice trailed off.

I studied Lela while we talked. She wore gold bangle bracelets halfway to her elbows on both arms, toe rings, and ankle bracelets with tiny bells attached all the way around. Her lipstick and fingernails were the exact color of her sari, and her eyes were heavily lined with kohl. Centered between them, high in her hairline, she wore a bright red bindi, a sign she was a married lady. She was the most feminine and exotic woman I had ever seen.

"Let me show you to your rooms," Lela announced, rising from the table and causing an immediate response from her staff. "Your luggage is already upstairs." She glided in her sari through the lobby, the dining room, and the halls, issuing orders in her melodic voice, her perfume and music from her bracelets trailing after her.

At the landing at the top of the stairs on the second floor, Lela stopped to catch her breath and to point out the two bathrooms at either end of the hallway. "There are no other hotel guests tonight. You will have private bathrooms, at least for today."

She opened a door to a room for Gemma and Dean to the left of the stairs, and then she walked me down the hall to another room at the other end of the corridor.

"Annie, dinner at eight," she said. "Please know that my husband and I are here for you. This is a lonely place for a young woman."

The room was small and white, but filled with late afternoon sunlight, the same golden light that had filled the dining room. The furniture was adequate—a single bed—but everything was immaculate. Lela's all-seeing eye was obvious upstairs, too. I looked out of the window and thought, amazed, *I'm going to sleep tonight in a five-hundred-year-old fort.*

I had been treated with nothing but kindness since I'd arrived, but I was overwrought, jet lagged, and simply sad. Everyone had done the best they could, from the Customs officer at the airport, Tedesu and his taxi, the desk clerk, the maître d' and the waiters at the Hotel Presidente, to Dean, Gemma, and Lela, but the truth was, I was disappointed with Mekele. It wasn't "African" enough for me, and I felt very far from home. I threw myself on the bed once I was alone, trying to come to some kind of acceptance of the situation, my arm over my eyes.

At dinner, Lela announced her proposal, addressing Gemma. "We will find Annie, you, and Dean homes tomorrow. I've asked around and there is something across town that might do for you and Dean, but I have another idea for Annie."

All three of us looked at her hopefully.

"I had a *tukol* built last year behind the hotel. You do know what a *tukol* is, Annie, don't you...the traditional Ethiopian house?"

"I think so," I said. "It's the round hut with the pointed straw roof?" We'd seen a glimpse of the hotel *tukol* as we'd driven up the mountain.

"Exactly," Lela continued. "Well, there's no one living in it. I built it for village government ceremonies, so it's very nice inside, but we haven't used it at all. There's no running water and no electricity, but my mechanic can hook up an outdoor gravity shower for you. You can come up here to use a bathtub with hot water when the hotel isn't busy."

"No running water?" I asked. "That means no toilet."

"On the side of the hotel there's a toilet room for the gardeners and the staff. I'll give you a key," Lela said, continuing as if the lack of running water was only a small detail. "There's a space for a small outdoor kitchen, and I can give you oil lanterns for light. I know a young girl who can help out with your cooking and washing, and my kitchen boys and I can teach her some simple European dishes. I'll bring her into the hotel and show her how to take care of you. There's even room to start a vegetable garden of your own."

A garden? It sounded like an awful lot of work, and I hadn't a clue how to begin. There weren't many home vegetable gardens in Manhattan or the suburbs of New York City.

"I'll send one of the boys down to invite you to dinner from time to time, so you won't always be alone. I think it's a good idea for you to live close to us. You'll need more company than a newly married couple."

Dean looked at Gemma with relief, then to me. I nodded to Dean and thanked Lela. It felt like the right thing to do.

"We'll go down to look at it after breakfast tomorrow," Lela said, pleased with herself. "I'll feel better knowing you're next door. These mountain people don't understand a young woman without a husband. I don't want the local men getting the wrong idea about you."

Dinner was as promised—homemade lasagna made with fresh tomato and meat sauce and long sheets of hand-rolled pasta. We had stuffed and deep-fried zucchini flowers, green beans, and chocolate ice cream for dessert.

"Did you make the ice cream here in your kitchen?" Gemma asked.

"Yes, my dear," Lela said. "There's nothing to it—cream, eggs, sugar, cocoa powder, ice, salt, and muscle power…all ingredients that you can find easily in Mekele. When you're settled, you must send your new houseboy for a cooking lesson." She spoke like a queen.

"I'll come for the cookery instruction. I'd like to learn as well," said Gemma, as imperiously as Lela.

The next morning, Dean and Gemma drove off in the Land Rover to see the Western-styled house Lela had found for them. The waiter from yesterday's tea and dinner, Ibrahim, brought a happy Daisy from the back of the hotel to the veranda.

"Miss Annie," he said, "M'dam Lela said I am to show you the *tukol*. Please, it is good for you to follow me now."

We walked along the hotel's back footpath, Daisy first, straining at her leash, Ibrahim next, in Western-styled trousers two sizes too large for him, cinched with a piece of rope at his narrow waist like a drawstring bag, and then me, stumbling over rocks and potholes in my sandals and long, peasant skirt.

"Careful for the many snakes and scorpions," Ibrahim warned. "It is why I carry this big stick. I will look out for you this day, but you will need to find your own stick. There are hyenas and vultures, but they will not bother you unless you are dead."

*Snakes and scorpions! Hyenas and vultures! What have I let myself in for?*

It was a round hut, maybe twenty-five feet across, made from mud, straw, and cow dung packed between supporting branches, clinging to the edge of a cliff and adjacent to the hotel. It had been freshly whitewashed and it sparkled in the sunlight. A porch wrapped all the way around it with pink bougainvillea climbing up each support, shaded by that distinctive pointed thatched roof over it all.

Inside, the single round room had also been painted white. The straw ceiling rose to twenty feet at its center and perhaps twelve feet at the perimeter. Decorative wide bands of dyed straw in red, black, yellow, and green, the colors of Africa, rose in concentric circles toward the center point. Small, rectangular windows with glass panes circled the room above my head. They let in the sun and created small rectangles of light that played across the packed dirt floor.

I went out to the cliff side of the hut and saw where an outdoor shower could go with some added privacy for me, and the perfect plot of land next to it for a small garden. I'd be able to shower and water my vegetables at the same time. The cliff dropped off abruptly ten feet past the *tukol*. The mountains looked uninhabited but for the hyenas, the vultures sailing on the air currents, and the baboons I saw on the cliffs directly below me. The residents of the entire mountainside would witness my most personal morning routine. I imagined squatting in the Extreme Chair yoga position and wondered what I would use for toilet paper.

Lela had been quite clear at dinner—there was no electricity, no plumbing or running water. It did have a pretty, overgrown garden with pink bougainvillea blossoms spilling over the rock walls as well as the porch supports, huge bursts of lavender flowering bushes, Bird of Paradise plants as high as the walls, and giant poinsettias the size of small trees with red flowers the size of dinner plates. A stand of jacaranda trees loaded with blue blossoms mostly hid the ground floor of the looming fort from view. Even from the second floor, it looked like I would be undetectable while the jacarandas were blooming.

The hut looked out over mountain after mountain and canyon after canyon, as far as I could see. It would be like living right on the rim of the

Grand Canyon, multiplied tenfold. The sky was immense. This dazzling setting would have to be the consolation prize for no bathroom.

When Gemma and Dean returned from their trip across town, they were excited with their find. We all now had new homes. After lunch, Lela's "boys" balanced our luggage on their heads and glided down the front steps. They carried mine down to the hut, with Gemma, Dean, Daisy, and me following. Gemma and Dean were curious to see my new home.

"It's round inside, too." Dean's eyes lit up. "Man, this is so groovy. With some cushions and a big, round coffee table, what a great place for a party." He looked up at the striped ceiling. "I really like this."

"Where will you sleep?" Gemma asked. "What will you sleep on?"

"My sleeping bag, I guess. And I brought a quilt from home."

"Where's the toilet?" Dean asked.

"Lela gave me the key. Come with me to check it out?"

We walked through the jacaranda trees and found a door set into the stone wall of the hotel at ground level. The key fit the lock, and we opened the door, took a look around, inhaled once, and backed out. It was nothing more than a hole in an oversized pan, like a metal paint pan without its roller. It sloped gradually on all sides to the center. It was filthy, coated with many layers of diarrhea, both dried and fresh. There was no toilet paper.

"I guess I'm supposed to squat over that hole." I frowned. "Maybe those ridges are there so my feet won't get dirty." I looked closely and, sure enough, there were slight indentations in the shape of footprints on either side of the black hole.

"You can't use that," said Gemma, backing out, her hand over her nose and mouth.

"It'll be easier to just go outside, lean out over the cliff, and stick your butt out," Dean laughed.

I wondered, again, what I would use for toilet paper.

"You'll be just fine," Gemma assured, peering at me, hoping that would be the case. I could tell from the look on her face she wasn't really convinced.

"Of course I will," I said, feeling the same way.

"Gemma, let's go," Dean nudged her. "We have to unpack." He turned to me, a touch of sympathy in his voice. "Tomorrow we'll start looking for a factory building together."

*Don't go*, I thought. *Don't leave me here.*

"We'll pick you up at ten," Dean said, as they waved goodbye.

Once I could no longer hear their Land Rover crunching down the gravel driveway and they were gone, really gone, I sank to the floor, my back against the curved wall. Forlorn, I looked around the empty *tukol* and broke apart. My crying came out of nowhere, pent up for two days, but, once loosened, the tears came as a relentless flood, the wails in giant gulps. I shocked myself by the sounds coming from my throat.

I had anticipated that setting up the factory and training the sewing machine operators in a foreign language would be difficult, but I hadn't considered my living arrangements would be so primitive. I looked around my new home, unprepared and afraid. I questioned my experience and abilities to make a success of this project, knowing Dean and Gemma were counting on me. I tried to feel better by imagining Jane Goodall, alone for months at a time in a leaking tent in the humid, dripping Tanzanian rain forest. It didn't help. Homesick and overwhelmed, I missed my family and my comfortable life in New York more than I would have ever imagined.

I angrily brushed the tears away, but they kept spilling. I held Daisy tight. I was having trouble breathing from the altitude—we were over seven thousand feet above sea level now—and gave myself a sore throat from trying to hold back the sobs. Most of all, I was mad at myself for this meltdown. I had what I'd longed for my entire childhood, maybe not exactly the way I had pictured it, but I was finally in Africa.

I could see from my window a young man watching the hut, leaning over the railing of the hotel veranda. He could hear me sobbing through the thin walls of the *tukol*. I knew, from the way he stood so still with his head cocked toward the sound of my weeping, how concerned he was. That only made it worse. I was completely furious that someone was feeling sorry for me. I crawled into my sleeping bag and Daisy curled around my head. I only wanted to fall into an oblivious nap for the rest of the afternoon. Instead, I found myself unable to sleep, thinking of home.

# 4/ A Soaring Heart: Whitestone, New York

I grew up in a good family, in a good neighborhood, where people lived good, upstanding lives. There was no alcoholism or drug addiction, no divorce, no rape or sexual abuse, no screaming or hitting, no smoking or cursing—not only in my own family, but in almost every other family I knew. It was a suburban Long Island world where everyone was white, middle class, and part of a family of four.

There were whispers I overheard between the mothers during Mah Jong games about the father of my best friend who might be cheating on his wife with his secretary. And more gossip about the father in the house next door who decided one morning that he wasn't going to work ever again, got back into bed, and never left it. Through his depression, and his ultimate death, his wife continued to design, sew, and sell hostess aprons to all the other neighborhood women—those frilly half-aprons women wore at late 1950s dinner parties that were featured in magazine advertisements for refrigerators and cereal, overly decorated with organza ruffles, satin ribbon bows, artificial cherries, or daisies.

The gossip about those suffering families was the only indication that life outside our home could be complicated and chaotic. In our house, my father worked uncomplainingly, up at dawn, home by six. He adored my mother; my mother appreciated my father and bowed to his wishes; and they both would have done anything, sacrificed everything, for my brother and me.

But, just as it's difficult to grow up unscathed by the devastation of a rough childhood, it's also not so easy to come from a good home. It's always there—safe, predictable, smothering, and beckoning. As a young woman, I had to work like hell to put some distance between my family and myself and to carve my own way out with my photographs, my books, and my dreams. I was lucky. I had my father behind me, always pushing me gently forward.

As a young girl, I played with Barbie dolls in the backyard, pretending they were mothers of toddlers, sharing a picnic, using a paper napkin as a picnic blanket. Barbie's bare feet never touched the grass. The imaginary children played close to their mothers, drank their milk, and ate only healthy food.

But sometimes I grew restless with my fantasy of perfect motherhood. Barbie then became Jane. The napkin, folded down the center and hung from a low branch, became a tent. I added my toy set of plastic, miniature African animals. I played with them under the hedges, imagining an African rainforest, and re-enacted scenes from Disney's *Wonderful World of Color* and *National Geographic* television specials.

I was the kind of ten-year-old who, alone in my bedroom with Degas ballerina sketches on the pale blue walls and lilac bushes framed in the window, watched myself sing "When You Wish Upon A Star" or "Someday My Prince Will Come" from Disney movies over and over again into my full-length mirror. I practiced heartache, hands clasped together at chest height, elbows out to the side—a perfect Snow White— and wished for a love that would heal my imaginary broken heart. But I also continued to clip and tape the images of Africa into my scrapbook and envisage a different kind of life for myself.

I was always my father's daughter; my ability to dream big and believe in myself was fostered by him. He made his living as a photographer who took aerial progress photos for major construction projects in the New York City area. On occasional school holidays or weekends, he took my brother and me up in the helicopters he hired to get his shots.

From the air, we saw the World's Fair go up, the Long Island Expressway snake its way the length of Long Island, the Throgs Neck Bridge, Lincoln Center, many Manhattan skyscrapers, and the twin towers of the World Trade Center. He would ask the pilot to set the helicopter down right on a roof of an office building in Manhattan or in the middle of a bridge under construction. My dad would walk us as close to the edge of the site as safely possible—my brother and I had our very own extra-small hard hats—and he'd proudly show us the view, his arms spread wide as if he'd created it just for us. Looking down from our vantage point, he'd tell us all those skyscrapers surrounding us were first somebody's dream.

"If you can dream it, you can make it happen. Your dreams tell you what you're capable of. If you didn't have it in you to attain your dreams, you wouldn't dream them in the first place."

I was the oldest. He'd put his hands on my shoulders and tell me, "You have a soaring heart, Ann. Never be afraid of your soaring heart."

Once a year, on a Saturday in the spring, my father took me, without my mother or brother, into Manhattan for afternoon tea at the Plaza Hotel. We would both dress up, he in a dark suit and tie, and me in my best dress, party shoes, white anklets, and gloves. "Our date," he'd call it. We walked across the lobby to the Palm Court and every year the same maître d' welcomed us, kissed the back of my hand, and called me Mademoiselle. He sat us at a perfect table and pulled out the chair he intended for me. I practiced my most ladylike manners and was very aware of the smiles we received from the waiters and the hotel guests seated around us.

I was very proud of my handsome father and pleased to have his undivided attention in such a public way. I knew, even as a young girl, I was the most fortunate of daughters.

After tea, we walked to the alcove in the lobby where a larger-than-life portrait of Eloise hung. Eloise was the central character from my favorite children's book, *Eloise at the Plaza*, by Kay Thompson. In the story, she lived upstairs in the Plaza's guest rooms and had comical adventures with the staff and the guests. Above all else, I loved the light-hearted illustrations. The canvas in the Plaza lobby had been painted by the original illustrator of the book, Hilary Knight.

I'd stare up at the huge painting and dance before it, pretending Eloise and I were friends, dancing together, only dimly conscious of the adults bustling back and forth through the revolving doors behind me. My father would sit beside me on a black and white striped satin, upholstered chair set at a right angle to the portrait, an exact replica of the chair in the portrait. He crossed his long legs, settled in for a visit of indeterminable length, and watched me indulgently until I was ready to go home.

Many years later, I stayed as a guest at the Plaza as an adult. After checking in, I walked across the busy lobby to revisit the Palm Court. I could hear the tinkling of harp music above all the noise and the bustle. There, at the podium, was the same maître d' from my childhood and, standing at attention along the potted palms, were many of the same waiters.

The maître d' recognized me. "Ah, Mademoiselle. How nice to see you again. I see you are all grown up." He kissed the back of my hand as he had when I was a child and asked after my father. "You were a very lucky little girl to have had such a father," he said.

Our father encouraged my brother and me to develop our interests, not just with his words, but with his time and attention. Whatever it was that interested us, we were given the best equipment and the lessons we needed to excel at it. Whether it was guitar, ice-skating, sailing, waterskiing, horseback riding, painting, bicycle racing, or dance classes, we were supported with both his money and his time.

When my artistic ability was recognized in the fourth grade, my dad started a new father-daughter tradition. Every Saturday morning at ten o'clock, we'd drive to the local art supply store. I could buy one—and only one—item. Sometimes I'd choose a special soft pencil or a charcoal stick I had never tried, sometimes a pad of watercolor paper, or a complete set of tempura paints. The cost never mattered to him.

My brother had his special time with our dad on Sunday mornings. They left for Manhattan before dawn so my brother could participate in the citywide bike races in Central Park. My dad was the official timekeeper. One night a week they went to the neighborhood bike shop. My brother could buy one new part for the racing bicycle they were building together from scratch.

One Friday night, my father came home from his studio pulling a trailer, a sixteen-foot fiberglass sailboat with a centerboard, a captain's hat, and a paperback instruction manual on sailing. There had been no discussion beforehand with my brother and me, and it seemed like a miracle that late spring evening when he pulled into the driveway with a boat. The next morning, we launched it into Little Neck Bay with optimistic expectations, my dad put on his new captain's hat, we opened the manual, and taught ourselves to sail.

One of the things we liked to do in the late spring, before the water was warm enough for swimming, was to sail across the bay to La Guardia Airport and drop anchor at the base of the runways. We would lie on our backs for entire afternoons as the planes took off, soaring and thundering perhaps thirty feet above us, one after the other, making the air, the water, the boat, our voices, and our stomachs vibrate. As each plane lifted off, there would be that moment, that tiny, cold moment of fear I felt in the pit of my stomach, when I'd wonder if this would be the time the plane would crash into the water on top of us. That fear, that moment of possible danger, my heart pounding in my chest, was the thrill and the whole point of those afternoons for me. I loved it, courted it, and wanted more.

Our sailing came in handy when I grew into a teenager, seeing in a whole new way the neighborhood boys I'd grown up with. When I would ask permission to go on a date, my father would offer an alternative.

"Why don't you just invite him to come sailing with us on Saturday? You'll have a lot more fun out on the water than cooped up in a movie theater. Invite him to come for Chinese food with us afterward. My treat."

Those boys always happily accepted. We were the only family in our neighborhood with a sailboat. During those afternoons out in the bay, I often thought the boys enjoyed my father's company more than mine. He put them to work dockside, included them in his captain's orders, and listened to them respectfully during the lulls between wind and direction changes. The unspoken message was that I was a good girl who was carefully watched.

The boys who asked me out didn't mind that they rarely got past first base. They had a fun day on the water, they were treated like men and got a free dinner out in a restaurant. I got a squeeze on my shoulder or an awkward goodnight kiss on my cheek while my parents sat in the front seat of the car.

And what was my mom's role in all this? She was our biggest fan and cheerleader. She sewed the canvas boat cushions for the sailboat and packed hundreds of tuna sandwiches for our weekend sails. In the fall, she drove me to my horseback riding lessons and sat patiently in the car with the heater on. When winter came, she made us hot cocoa and cinnamon toast on school Snow Days, bundled us up in our snowsuits, and dragged us on our sleds to the gentle hills of the snow-covered golf course behind our house.

She drove my brother and me to the skating rink and watched us, wearing her winter car coat and leather gloves and sitting on the freezing metal bleacher seats as we skated back and forth across the ice. We learned to skate and then dance, forward and backward, stop on the edges of our blades, spin, do figure eights, waltz. How bored she must have been, and how cold. When we were through, exhilarated from the exercise and the cold, she met us with hot cocoa from the concession stand and unlaced our skates in her lap, always telling us how well we'd done. And she reached down without a word to pick up the gloves we thoughtlessly let drop between the benches. She was a rock, always there, unwavering in her love for all of us and in the belief that we were "the best"—her words—at everything we tried.

My brother and I walked home from school together for lunch and she always, without fail, had a good meal waiting for us on our white Formica, hexagonal kitchen table. Within a week of its arrival, I had scored a deep groove in the top with a mat knife the first time I tried to cut the frame for a picture. She never said a word about it. Nothing she could have ever said would have made me feel guiltier than sitting down to breakfast, lunch, and dinner, day after day, year after year, seeing that scratch beside my place setting.

Like most families, we watched TV together after dinner. The Women's Rights Movement of the late sixties took place directly in our living room as Bella Abzug, Betty Friedan, and Gloria Steinem blazed with righteous indignation across our television screen. As the TV news reported women's office sit-ins, demonstrations, the new birth control pill, and bra burnings, I looked from my mother to my father. I knew that my mother was essential to the well-being of our family, but I also knew I didn't want to model my adult life after hers.

The world was being transformed before my eyes, and I wanted to be a part of it. My choices, I promised myself, would be unlimited.

I valued my father's intelligence, his attention, and his example more than I did my mother's selfless devotion. I knew, even as a pre-teen, that I could never just stand on the sidelines and cheer someone else's accomplishments.

My father was a reader, and I became an avid one, too. He had three or four library books by his bedside and another stack by his armchair in the living room at all times. When I picture my dad now, he is sitting in a webbed lawn chair in the slanted, late afternoon sun on our front porch. He's in his everyday uniform of khaki chinos, tan leather Topsiders, a red plaid shirt—short-sleeved cotton in the summer or long-sleeved flannel in the fall—his long legs crossed at the knees. He always had an open book on his lap. He read everything. He believed books opened worlds and, if my brother and I were readers, we could go anywhere with our imaginations.

During the school year, every Wednesday night was library night, not only for my brother and me, but for any of the neighborhood kids. They knew if they wanted to go with us they just had to wait for us by our garage after dinner—6:30 p.m. on the dot. Dad would take whoever showed up.

He was on friendly terms with the librarians at our neighborhood library as well as the one near his studio. Every week, he'd ask the librarian if she had any new book recommendations on Africa for me. Sometimes he came home from work with an old *National Geographic* or a *Life* magazine I could cut apart. When I got older he took me into the city, to the second-hand book stores on University Place in lower Manhattan. I searched through the outdoor bins for books on Africa, and he'd search for first editions of any kind.

I never thought of myself as spoiled. We were often told that children should have what they need and not what they want. We never got comic books or cheap toys from the grocery store. We did get the most expensive ice skates, the lessons, the imported Italian bike parts, tea at the Plaza, and a sailboat. Everything came with the unstated belief that we were worth the investment, we deserved the best, and it was expected that we would succeed.

My father took my ambitions seriously, and I knew that if he did, then I could, too. I was this little girl with her African dreams, who looked down on all of Manhattan from the top floor of an unfinished skyscraper, holding her father's hand, believing the whole world could be hers. And she learned to listen to what her father called her soaring heart.

# 5/ Amira: Mekele, Ethiopia

I didn't sleep well that first night alone in my *tukol*; some creature rustled in the thatched roof, and hyenas howled and yipped in the valley below. As soon as dawn began to break as a strip of lavender-gray above the mountain's black jagged silhouette, I wrapped myself in my sleeping bag, walked with Daisy to the edge of the cliff behind the hut, and watched the day begin. As the sun rose to meet the mountaintops, the far-off cliffs became lit with a warm golden light. Not a soul moved, neither human nor animal.

There were no other huts like mine with signs of life stirring and morning cook fires sending smoke plumes into the sky, no farmers tending fields of vegetables, no predators trotting back to their caves, sated and ready for sleep, no vultures coasting, soaring—nothing but the brightening mountains above and shadowed valleys below. And the sky, always the sky, dark as ink or bleached white by the sun, as much a presence in the landscape as the cliffs. Feeling insignificant and lonely, I hugged Daisy close.

Amira came, wrapped from head to knees in a traditional white gauze shawl and covered with road dust. She was so thin from the recent famine that the contours of her jawbone, cheekbones, and eye sockets stood out sharply against her brown skin stretched taut across her face. This was the younger sister of the kitchen boy, Abrahim. He had been ordered by Lela to bring her to the hotel with him this morning.

Once the sun had risen, I'd watched from my mountain perch as they picked their way along a footpath through two nearby mountains, the first moving creatures in the landscape. They climbed the hill to the hotel and turned onto the dirt path toward the *tukol*. I went around and met them by the front door.

Amira reminded me of a frightened deer, with a deer's deep brown, expressive eyes, and skin the color of a deer's coat. She was so shy and skittish she was unable to look directly at me, staring down at the floor or gazing at the animals. Her eyelids quivered and her hands shook. She seemed ready to bolt, but her brother pushed her forward so she stood directly in front of me. Daisy barked once, half-heartedly, and sniffed at Amira's dusty legs and callused, bare feet. Amira and Abrahim carried with them an odor of spices, of red pepper and sweat that was new to Daisy, and intriguing.

"Miss Annie, remember me? I am Abrahim from yesterday. This, she is my sister, Amira. M'dam Lela say Amira is to be your housemaid and cook. She has thirteen years. She has Amharic only, no English, but she hard worker."

*She looks eleven. She should be in school...not working as someone's housemaid.*

I looked around the empty hut and wondered what she could possibly do all day to keep busy, but I trusted Lela's judgment and agreed to hire her. Her brother asked that she should be paid twelve U.S. dollars a month. It was a small amount to me, but I sensed it would mean everything to her family. If she could try to keep the *tukol* clean and pest-free, cook breakfast and dinner, and wash clothes in a home with no running water, then I would see that she was fed well and would send food home to her family.

Throughout this transaction, Amira said nothing, but soon, feeling more comfortable, she began to peek from behind her shawl, stealing furtive glances at me and her surroundings. She stood perfectly still, her face blank, her demeanor gentle, but her eyes told the story. She was hungry and desperate. Behind the hunger, I saw the smallest glint of hope for this lucky opportunity and I warmed to her. I already felt calmer in her presence.

"Abrahim, please tell Amira she is welcome, and I'm sure she will do a good job." I'd never had a maid of my own and took my cue from my mother and her relationship with Willie May, our family's cleaning lady.

They were turning to leave when we noticed two small boys running up the footpath to the *tukol*, holding a full sack of grain between them. When they reached us, they thrust the bag at Abrahim, who translated their excited Amharic.

"These boys have catched a female baby dik-dik in the mountains. It has no mother, they say, but, Miss Annie, I do not believe this. They say they know you have come to live in Mekele and they want you to have her for a pet. They know all Americans like pets. She will not get very big, only to your knee. The dik-dik is the smallest antelope. Come and look at her in the bag."

The boys came forward and the baby dik-dik's head appeared from the open end of the sack. I looked all the way in. She was no bigger than two hands cupped together, with long, twig-like legs that looked like they could snap as easily as a chicken wishbone. She had a smooth, caramel-colored coat, with a black nose and what looked like black, Cleopatra eye makeup outlining her honey-colored eyes. She was feminine, curious and, even with her head peeking out from the sack, she carried herself with a regal air. I fell in love.

I took the dik-dik from the bag and held her against my chest. She folded her long legs delicately beneath her torso and relaxed in my arms.

"I'll take her," I said. "Tell the boys I'm happy they've brought me this gift."

"No, no, Miss Annie," Abrahim shook his head. "She is not a gift. The boys want ten U.S. dollars for her."

"Oh...of course. Tell them, of course, I'll pay them ten dollars. We have a deal."

I paid them, aware that I was giving them a great deal of money for a baby animal most likely stolen from its mother.

"What does she eat?" I asked.

Abrahim questioned the boys and then translated. "She eats leaves, grasses, flowers, and coffee berries. It will be easy to feed her." He looked at the tiny creature nestled in my arms, and his grim expression softened. "You must keep her in the *tukol* until you can find a rope and a goat bell for her, for she will not know this is her house."

"Can you help me name her? I want to call her something Ethiopian."

Abrahim translated my request to Amira, who had been silently watching the transaction from behind her white gauze shawl.

"Negiste." Abrahim relayed to me Amira's first spoken word in my presence.

"Does it have a meaning in English?" I asked.

"It means 'Queenie' or 'Princess,' Miss Annie."

"Perfect." I looked straight into Amira's beautiful face and smiled, but she turned her eyes back to the ground.

Abrahim had spent more time than he had planned at the *tukol* and anxiously said goodbye. "We go to the hotel now. Tomorrow, or today later, Amira, she is coming to your *tukol* for working. Today, M'dam Lela teach her cleaning the rooms and cooking American dishes." Abrahim spoke to Amira in a rough, hurried voice and turned her away from the door by pulling at her arm. As she followed after him up the back footpath to the hotel, she looked over her shoulder and gave Daisy a small, wan smile.

Gemma and Dean pulled up in the Land Rover shortly afterward. It had already been a busy morning with two sets of guests, but I was very happy to see them, too, so early in the day.

"We've come for breakfast at the hotel. Join us," Gemma commanded, like a British royal. She took the tiny antelope from me. "Oh, Dean, darling. Look at it. I want one, too," she crooned. "What is it? Where did it come from?"

"These boys just brought her to my door. You must have passed them on the road up the hill. I thought they were giving me a welcome gift, but it turned out they wanted money. It's a she—a baby dik-dik. I'm calling her Negiste—Princess. And I just hired a maid."

"Good Lord, you settle in quickly," Gemma exclaimed. Dean looked relieved that I was happier this morning and seemed reconciled to my new home.

I dressed quickly and met them in the hotel dining room, hungry for breakfast. Neither Gemma nor I felt ready to take on housekeeping and cooking chores quite yet. The toast was cut from home-baked bread, the eggs were fresh from the chickens in the yard, with yolks a deep orange, and the freshly roasted Ethiopian coffee was the best I'd ever tasted. With food in my stomach, company in the *tukol*, and a baby antelope to raise, things looked brighter.

Lela came in from the kitchen, perfumed, made-up to perfection, draped in a lime green silk sari with a gold stripe at the hem and gold sandals on her feet.

"You've hired Amira, I hear. Very good," Lela said, a hand on my shoulder. "I will work with her today. She's in the kitchen now with the cook. Already I can see she is a fast learner like her brother. She'll become irreplaceable to you in a very short time."

"She's very young," I said. "I like her very much, but the more I think about it, hiring her doesn't seem right. D'you think I should visit her parents to make sure it's okay?"

"Annie, they'll be grateful that Amira will be bringing money to the family. They are lucky. There are very few jobs in Mekele, especially for a girl."

"She doesn't go to school?"

"Poor girls in Ethiopia don't go to school. They are married off young."

"How young?" I asked.

"Amira's age—thirteen or fourteen. As soon as they can bear children."

"How awful." The fourteen-year-old girls I knew read *Seventeen* magazine, strutted in their gogo boots, and dreamed of making it onto the cheerleading squad.

*I'll teach her to read*, I thought. It was something I could do to lessen the guilt about hiring a child to cook and clean. *I'll teach her to speak, read, and write in English, and then she will have those skills long after I've left Mekele.*

Gemma, Dean, and I spent the morning shopping for household items—pots; pans; grates and metal oven boxes for our fires; dishes and silverware; soap; traditional Ethiopian baskets that were smaller versions of my striped, straw roof; towels and pillows; two rough, hand-carved benches for me; a table, chairs, and a bed for Gemma and Dean. Everything was of the poorest quality, manufactured in Addis or imported from other African countries. The Mekele market smelled intensely of Africa—spices, rotting fruit, and dirt.

We walked along the open market, stopping to purchase onions and tomatoes, squash, coffee, matches, sugar, salt and pepper, just as I had imagined the day before, and causing a sensation among the Ethiopian women sitting behind their meager pyramids of produce.

Tailors and a sandal maker had set up their ancient treadle sewing machines in front of their shops. A barber conducted business from a rickety chair placed on the same stretch of sidewalk. A rough butcher shop took up one corner, and an entire skinned cow hung from a hook in the ceiling, crawling with flies. The shop, deep in shadows, buzzed with the sound; we could hear it from the sidewalk. Hundreds of the insects had been trapped by flypaper that hung alongside the cow, and many more long-dead and desiccated ones had fallen in piles on the dirt floor.

All cuts of beef were sold by the kilo for the same price and wrapped in old newspaper. Mekele commerce took place in the open. Everyone stared as we passed. Smiling and nodding nervously to everyone, we received very little genuine warmth in return.

We stopped in at the general store and introduced ourselves to the owner, a dour, middle-aged Indian man with a full mustache, graying beard, and a brown turban. He was barely visible behind the counter in his dark and dusty shop, sitting glumly on a stool, guarding his meager inventory and the mostly empty shelves. Dust motes danced in the slices of sunlight that penetrated the gloom.

He had a small amount of an astonishing number of items for sale— fluorescent pink polyester cardigan sweaters, Keds sneakers with no laces, matches, cocoa powder, tin buckets, lunch pails, fry pans, and plastic jugs strung on cord across the ceiling. Forty-gallon drums of gasoline and five-gallon, square, plastic containers of kerosene and paraffin lined the walls.

"Look, Dean, darling," Gemma pointed to a small display of canned peaches stacked neatly on a shelf that held nothing else. "Let's buy some."

"We don't have a can opener," Dean reminded her, his voice dripping with irony. "You don't have one for sale, do you?" he asked the Indian shopkeeper, who shook his turbaned head morosely.

When Dean pulled up at the *tukol*, I was surprised to find Amira sitting on the patch of grass in the front yard, playing quietly with Daisy and Negiste. They seemed spellbound by her, sensing her gentleness, and followed her every move with their eyes. We had driven right into the scene in *Snow White* where the woodland animals help with the housework.

I left my bundles on the front porch and joined them in the yard, but the magic disappeared as soon as I'd opened the car door. Amira quickly stood, afraid she'd been caught playing instead of working. When I joined them, she busied herself with brushing the grass and dirt from the back of her white dress and shawl.

Loyal Daisy came to greet me, and Negiste bounded off to the garden and interested herself in pulling up tufts of grass and deadheading spent blossoms. She never needed the rope and bell. From that first day, Daisy and Negiste followed Amira wherever she went.

"Come," I said to Amira, beckoning her to the *tukol* door. Her first English word.

"Come." She repeated it tentatively. "Come."

It was a beginning.

Together we carried the new wooden benches inside and set them against the curved walls to make a kitchen area, then stacked them with the new dishes and pots. She was thrilled with all the items from town, an inconceivable bounty. She happily unwrapped the newspaper bundles of vegetables and spices and piled them in the new baskets. We stood back and admired our decorating.

"Come," Amira said, and she led me out the back door and proudly showed off the small charcoal fire she had started and, beside it, an overturned Coca Cola crate meant to be a work surface and cutting board.

Together we had created a kitchen.

"Let's make lunch." I mimed eating the way the Addis street orphans had—left hand cupped as a plate, right hand bringing imaginary food from it to my mouth with my fingers.

"Lunch," she responded, understanding. Her second English word.

She took a new, red plastic bowl, a knife, fork, plate, and a dented frying pan, an onion, a sweet potato, salt, a yellow squash, two eggs, a bit of butter folded in a newspaper page, and a large plastic jug of filtered water she had carried from the hotel kitchen for us. She set everything up on the wooden crate. She melted some butter in the new pan on a grate over the fire, washed, chopped, and fried the vegetables, added the eggs, and made an omelet— Lela's first cooking lesson of the morning. She set it before me on the back doorstep, standing close by, expressionless, stealing glances as I took a forkful and tasted. It was delicious. Finally, she sought my eyes and smiled.

It didn't feel right to eat while she watched. She had probably not eaten a thing yet that day. I sat the plate on the step, went inside to our new bench and the stacks of dishes, and came out with another plate and fork. I divided the omelet into two and slid one half onto the second plate for her. She was surprised, but accepted the plate and ate hungrily. She kept looking up toward the hotel, as if checking to see if Lela was watching from the verandah.

We were off to a good start, Amira and I. She could keep a fire going, had been taught to purify our cooking and drinking water, and how to cook an omelet, but she hadn't yet been taught how to wash dishes to Lela's standards. I found her on the footpath, scrubbing the fry pan and plates with pebbles. I shook my head and pointed to the plastic water jug. She looked at me, startled, not understanding, and I could only pantomime washing the dishes with the water from the jug.

Abrahim arrived just then to bring Amira back up to the hotel for the afternoon's lessons. I explained to him that I wanted Amira to wash the dishes with purified water. He grabbed her arm and shook it hard, speaking angrily to her in Amharic. Then he turned to explain to me, spitting his words, hissing like a snake.

"She is a stupid girl with stupid ways. I am sorry, Miss Annie. Our mother, a stupid woman, she cleans the bowls and the cooking pot with small rocks. We have no water for washing things, only for drinking. Amira, her job is carry water from town to our *tukol* in the mountain. It is a long way, and the full jug is heavy. Water is precious. This is all she knows. She will learn correct ways from M'dam Lela, and she will not wash dishes with rocks next time."

"I understand," I said. "But, Abrahim, please don't be angry with her, don't yell at her like you did, and please don't call her stupid, or your mother either. Tell M'dam Lela that Amira made a very good lunch and helped me set up our kitchen."

"I will tell her," Abrahim said, chastised but still shooting murderous glances at his sister.

He remembered something else.

"Miss Annie, we have heard in the kitchen that a poor nun has come to Mekele from America."

"A poor nun?" I asked. "Who is she?"

"It is *you*, Miss Annie," he shouted, grinning. "*You* are the poor nun."

"Me? A poor nun?"

"Yes, because you do not have a husband, like the nuns. And because your skirt is long and old and has patches, and your shoes show your feet, like mine."

A poor nun! I was horrified.

My hippie wardrobe, which I believed to be the height of seventies fashion, had been lovingly cultivated and packed so carefully back in New York. It consisted of ankle-length, patch-worked or embroidered skirts, Roman gladiator sandals, short-sleeved peasant blouses from assorted third world countries, and a distressed denim jean jacket. The people in town had seen and judged me through their own experience of the world. I could, indeed, be a poor nun come to Mekele.

Late that afternoon, when Dean and Gemma came back for me, I told them the gossip from town. They laughed and explained. Western television, movies, and magazines never reached Mekele. The people in Ethiopia understood the East Indians who owned the shops and lived in their midst, with their women wrapped in bright, shiny saris and golden musical jewelry. The only American or European foreigners—*ferenjis*—these northern, highland Ethiopians had ever seen were the rare, intrepid tourist, scientist, or explorer, dressed as if on safari, in khaki shorts or trousers, many-pocketed vests, and their feet well-shod in brown leather camping boots and wool socks.

Gemma remembered a tailor's shop we had passed by in town that had dusty safari clothing displayed on the inside walls, and a narrow shoe store with a small selection of boxed, imported shoes. She suggested we drive back to town to buy me a new wardrobe. Yes, I agreed. It was much better to be thought an explorer than a poor nun. I went on another spending spree, outfitting myself in baggy khaki shorts; white, gray, and olive-green T-shirts; wool socks; and tan camping boots, all in the smallest men's sizes, all swimming on me.

"These boots are the best in Mekele," the shop owner said proudly as he laced them on my feet. "No snake can bite you on the ankle in these boots."

I packed away my flowing, hippie garments and stepped into a new persona—the African explorer/adventurer, confidently striding across the continent. But that's all it was, a new persona, just as the flower child wardrobe had been a different one. Inside, I was a product of suburbia—ruffled hostess aprons, backyard playgrounds, Barbie dolls, dinner on the table at six o'clock sharp. With the wind blowing from another direction, I could just as easily have ended up with a hostess apron tied around my own waist.

# 6/ Andiamo: Mekele, Ethiopia

I was ready for Dean and Gemma when I heard the Land Rover make its way up the hill and into the courtyard shortly after dawn. I'd had a bad night—little sleep, bad dreams, afraid to leave the *tukol* to pee during the night—and I was relieved to see them.

Dean had a surprise. He'd found a building for our factory.

We drove down the mountain and across the town, passing the shopkeepers on the main street preparing for business. Women were setting up fresh produce displayed in baskets or piled in pyramids on sheets of old newspapers or tarpaulins laid out on the floor.

On the outskirts of town, we pulled up to a compound walled in on four sides, and, at the sound of Dean's horn, an old *askiri* wrapped in a blanket opened the gates to our new factory.

The building was once a coffee bean warehouse, but it had been abandoned for a number of years. It was a cinder-block structure that sat in the middle of the compound—gray, long, and squat, no more than four unpainted walls and a corrugated tin roof, with electricity. Small, square windows marched evenly beneath the roofline. Off to the right was the outhouse—three attached cinder-block toilet stalls with three steps up to wood doors and small, glassless windows above them for ventilation.

In front of the warehouse grew a huge flame tree with wide, splayed branches, brilliant red blossoms, and dense foliage. Large stones, painted white, led from the compound gates and circled the tree, delineating a driveway from the rest of the dirt surrounding the building. Nothing else grew except tufts of dry grass.

"I think this will work for us," Dean said, opening the front door.

The three of us stood in the doorway and took in the desolate building. It was dusty and bleak, but in fairly good condition, and Dean was right, it would work. It only needed a good sweeping—floors, walls, and ceiling—but I didn't want to see the condition of the outhouses. Dean promised to hire someone to clean, and we discussed possible layouts of the factory. In this, Dean allowed me to take the lead.

"We need to build or find long tables—one for sorting leather hides, one for cutting, another on the left side for bundling the cut pieces. Then, on the right, we'll need one for inspecting and another for packing and shipping. The sewing machines can go down the center."

I sounded like I knew what I was talking about and perhaps I did know a little, but I was still terrified.

"We can run the power to the sewing machines from those rows of industrial lights hanging from the ceiling. We also need shelves along the back wall for storing the finished garments."

"Dean, darling, can we build a picnic table for under the flame tree?" Gemma asked. "A shady place for lunch."

It was a good idea. I could picture it—the days and weeks ahead of us, the lunches in the shade, and the casual talks with our sewers. I felt more confident and more optimistic.

Dean drove off to find a carpenter who could build what we needed, leaving me to mark out the layout by scuffing my new boots in the dirt floor. He came back in less than an hour with a tall, thin, barefoot man swathed in white cotton, who took measurements with a pencil stub and a grubby piece of paper already covered with numbers and rough sketches.

"When can you start?" Dean asked him in Amharic.

"Now."

"When will you be finished?"

"The tables, tomorrow afternoon. The shelves, one day more."

"Chairs," Gemma suddenly remembered.

"Can you build us some chairs?" Dean asked the carpenter.

"How many?"

Dean looked at me, but I didn't have an answer.

"Twenty?" I suggested.

He turned to the carpenter. "Can you build twenty chairs for the sewing machines and twenty small benches?"

The man nodded and spoke.

"That will take four more days and he needs an assistant," Dean interpreted.

He went to shake the carpenter's hand, but the man had begun a deep bow—a bow for a monarch. He was profoundly grateful for the work. He continued to bow as he backed out the door.

Now we needed sewing machines and tailors, cutters, and sorters. We drove to the marketplace and approached the men stitching at machines in front of their shops or set up on the sidewalk. Dean spoke to them in Amharic, describing the new factory, offering jobs and wages starting the next day. The men seemed neither excited nor skeptical, and Dean walked away from these exchanges unsure of the outcome.

We took lunch again at the hotel with Lela, who looked pointedly at my new safari attire and my boots, but said nothing. She was beautifully made-up and draped in yet another sari. We drove back to the factory to oversee the carpenter and his assistant who had already brought up tools and lumber and were sawing away in the courtyard when we arrived. A donkey grazed there, and a camel rested under the shade of the flame tree, its legs folded beneath it.

"Stay away from the camel," Dean advised. "They spit and they bite."

The rest of the day, we worked with the carpenter, and I stayed well away from the camel.

Dean and Gemma dropped me off at the *tukol* late in the afternoon. I faced an evening alone there, with the light of two paraffin lamps and nothing to do. I could write to my parents, or watch the animals play. I was out behind the *tukol*, sitting at the edge of the cliff with Daisy and Negiste sniffing and foraging beside me, looking out over the jagged mountain peaks. Two vultures rode the air currents, swirling and dancing together in the sky. Nothing else moved. Amira had left for the day, leaving for home as soon as Dean and Gemma dropped me off. She had a long walk home up the other side of the valley and she needed to do as much of it as she could while it was still light.

I heard an automobile engine make its way up the hill to the hotel, turn left on the footpath to my *tukol*, idle by my front door, and then cut off. I walked around to the front to see who had arrived.

It was the handsome man who had been standing on the hotel verandah, listening to me crying my first night in Mekele. He smiled a big, bright-white smile when he saw me come around the side of the *tukol* to the driveway. He slammed the driver's-side door of his forest green, battered, old Citroën with his hip and held out a glass casserole dish covered with a faded dishtowel.

He was tall and thin, in faded Levis and a tangerine and white plaid, cowboy-styled shirt. He had a two- or three-day growth of beard, dark brown hair almost to his shoulders, and gentle green eyes. Although he was good-looking, he didn't seem to know it, and there was a tender quality to him I was drawn to.

"Anna, my name is Matteo Manfriando," he said. "I live in Mekele, in that house down the hill. *Per favore*, excuse my English. It is not very good, because I am Italian, but I was born in Addis. My family has lived in Ethiopia for thirty years."

He held the dish out. "Look…my mother has sent supper for you. They are stuffed peppers. They come from our garden. My mother, she wants you to have a meal tonight from our family. She is a good cook and she is worried about you. She doesn't want you to be alone in this *tukol* and hungry. Have you eaten dinner?"

Amira had left me a fried onion omelet…yet another omelet. "No, I haven't eaten and I'm starving."

"I can stay and eat with you," Matteo offered. "*Perché no?* Is better, no, to take your meal with another person?"

I peeked beneath the dishcloth. The peppers looked and smelled delicious. I clapped my hands, but held myself back from actually squealing with joy—stuffed peppers, one of my favorite dishes, covered with melted and browned mozzarella cheese. I took the glass dish from him and felt it was still warm.

"I don't have a table or chairs," I said, remembering.

"No problem. We sit on the step," Matteo said. "My mother, she also sent these." He pulled two knives and forks from his back pocket and sat down. He patted the space beside him.

"Come, sit," he said.

He handed me a fork and knife and the dishcloth to use as a napkin. "*Mangiare!* Let's eat!"

We shared the dish of peppers, eating with pleasure, making conversation, and watching the mountains turn gold from the lowering sun. Daisy begged for bites and Negiste curled up at my feet.

"You like it?" Matteo asked.

"Very much. It reminds me of my grandmother's cooking. She was a wonderful cook, too."

"Look, Anna. You can see my house from here, and the garden," he said, pointing to a compound below me. We could see the roof of the small house and a large vegetable garden to the side.

"Are you more happy today?" he asked. "Is today better? You were crying in the *tukol* the other night. I heard you from the veranda, but, don't worry, it was only me. No one could hear you in the dining room."

I smiled, relieved. It was exactly what I had been worried about.

"The other night, I wanted to tell you this, Anna—it will be okay. This is new and strange for you—Mekele, Addis, Africa. It is very different from New York, America."

"Will it really be okay?"

"You'll meet new people and learn about Ethiopia. You and I, we can be friends. I am here, just down the hill. I want to help you. *Per favore*, come to lunch tomorrow...*Venite a pranzo di domain*. My mother will make you a fantastic meal—the big meal of the day for Italians is lunch."

"I'll be working tomorrow at the factory. It's our first day," I said, truly sorry. "I don't think there will be time."

Matteo gave a short laugh. "For sure, you will have a lunch break and time for a *reposo*, a siesta...three or four hours. It's the Ethiopian custom, and an Italian one. Don't worry. I will pick you up at the factory at noon and take you back at four."

He seemed to know a lot about me—my name, where I was from, what I was doing in Mekele, and even where the new factory was, but, rather than worry me, I found it a comfort. Now that I had eaten and felt relaxed in his company, I realized how attractive Matteo was.

"It was nice of you to visit me," I said, rising. We were through eating. We had scraped our forks over the last bits of burned cheese along the sides of the glass dish, and I suddenly felt shy. It had been tiring to speak so slowly in English and keep my sentences short and simple so Matteo could follow. And he had to be exhausted as well from the effort it took to reach for his rarely used English. The sun was just beginning to set behind the mountains.

"Thank your mother for me for sending you with dinner. And thank you for the invitation to lunch. I'll be happy to come. Let me just wash out the dish and the silverware."

"*Buono! Grazie!* You make me very glad," Matteo said.

Together we walked around to the back of the *tukol* to the outdoor kitchen. Amira had left a plastic jug of purified water, as Lela had instructed her. I squatted in the dirt and began to scrub the casserole dish and utensils with a Brillo-type pad bought in the marketplace, but Matteo took them away from me and washed them himself. Daisy licked at his face.

"I think I can do this better than you can," he said, smiling. "It is easier to do this in my house. We have a sink in the kitchen and water comes into the house. We have electric lights, too…even in Mekele." A joke.

When he got up to leave, he pressed his lips to my forehead—not really a kiss.

"*Non essere triste.* Don't be sad, Anna. This is a great adventure for you."

It was exactly the wrong thing to say to me at that moment, and I started to cry once again. The strangeness, the loneliness, my doubts, and homesickness overwhelmed me. He held me and patted me on the back, not sure what else to do. Then he had a better idea.

"*Avanti…Andiamo…*Let's go for a drive. I want to show you something *especiale*. Sure to make you feel better."

He held the car door open for me, and I slid in beside him, still sniffling, my nose running. My throat ached from the effort to hold in my sadness.

We drove out of town and left the dirt-packed roads to make our own path down a steep hill between the ruts and rocks. We stopped in an isolated ravine with a shallow, slow-moving stream at the bottom. It spread out with wide, muddy banks on either side, making it a perfect water hole. Matteo parked, cut the engine, and pantomimed "quiet" with a forefinger to his lips.

"*Aspetteremo…*Now, we wait."

He took my hand across the gearbox, and we both sat very still, waiting for something to happen. Within five minutes, animals began to appear toward us from the surrounding mountains to drink from the stream.

First came a lone civet cat, moving tentatively toward the stream. It was a strange-looking animal—a cat's body, but with short legs; a leopard's spotted fur; a long, pointed nose; and a furry platypus's wide tail. It twitched its ears and sniffed the air in our direction, smelling the diesel gas fumes. It looked directly at us in the car, although we were both sitting still. Then, sensing no danger from us, it lowered its head and lapped at the surface of the stream. It drank its fill and trotted off between the boulders and disappeared.

Next came a half dozen timid Thompson gazelles, their coats golden in the setting sun, and three large ibex antelope with their long, pointed horns. A few moments later, they were joined by miniature dik-dik, like Negiste, too numerous to count in the twilight.

We sat quietly in the car, not moving an inch. The animals drank and moved off into the canyons. The sun set suddenly and dramatically, the sky turning lavender, then purple, and the mountains disappeared into the blackest night.

This was it—the Africa of my childhood dreams. The animal photographs from my scrapbook had come to life right before my eyes.

"There used to be lions and elephants in northern Ethiopia, but not anymore. Maybe there are some in the south. Sometimes I see zebras here, but not often," Matteo said.

"Thank you for this, Matteo." I closed my eyes to seal the images into my memory. "I'd forgotten. This is why I'm here." He had given me the most precious gift.

"I come here to remind myself why I stay here, too," Matteo said, turning on the ignition and the headlights and heading the car back in the direction we had come. We bounced across rocks and gullies, and Matteo seemed to know his way through all the dark and emptiness. The boulders, the termite mounds, and the individual mountain silhouettes against the sky were like street signs to him, pointing him back to Mekele.

"I hope you will be happy here, Anna," he said when he dropped me off at my *tukol*. He came around to my side to open the door and help me out. "It will take time to get used to this life. Be patient. Any time you like, we can drive to the stream…and tomorrow I will pick you up for lunch."

He gave me a really passionate kiss then, his hands on both sides of my face, his tongue and the soft inside of his lips brushing against my open mouth. I stood there, leaning against the car door, surprised by the suddenness and the ferocity of it…the longing in it. I hadn't experienced those kinds of kisses before, or a man who asserted himself so confidently. I kissed him back, surprised I seemed to know how to respond.

"*Buono note*, Anna," he said, his hands on either side of my face. "I'll come for you tomorrow."

He got back in his car and drove off down the hill, leaving me in the driveway, stunned, with my hand over my mouth.

# 7/ Settling In: Mekele, Ethiopia

I was woken by Amira in the morning with a cup of chai tea while it was still dark, and it took a moment to remember where I was. Me! With a housemaid shaking me gently awake with a cup of tea in her hand as if I were a princess. I may have slept in a sleeping bag on a dirt floor, sharing it with all kinds of critters, and I would soon wash my face and brush my teeth from a gourd of freezing water, but I also got to drink my first cup of tea of the day in bed—ridiculous.

Amira must have started her walk from her family's *tukol* in the middle of the night. I didn't like it. Lela would tell me what time Ibrahim began work at the hotel, and what was the custom. Whatever the custom, I couldn't expose Amira to danger for twelve U.S. dollars a month.

Dean and Gemma pulled up to the *tukol* soon after the sun had risen completely over the mountains.

"Our first day," Dean called out from the driver's-side open window, chipper and optimistic, freshly shaven, smelling of cologne, and dressed for a workday in downtown Chicago—tie and all. Gemma was dressed in a gray tweed mini skirt, black leather knee-high boots, and a perfectly pressed white cotton blouse.

"I hope it's okay with you, but I have sort of a date for lunch," I announced from the back seat. "I met a nice man last night. I liked him."

Gemma whipped her head around. "Whaaat?"

"He invited me for lunch today with his family."

"Who is he?" Dean asked, curious.

"His name is Matteo Manfriando. His family lives near the hotel. He's from Addis, but his parents have retired here in Mekele. His father was the personal accountant to the emperor."

"I don't know who they are," Dean mused, rubbing his chin.

"You really *do* work fast," Gemma observed.

As we drove through the marketplace, I asked if we could stop so I could shop for a gift for Matteo's mother. Gemma and I ducked in between donkeys and women from the countryside squatting in the dirt, setting up their produce and spices on sheets of old newspaper or plastic groundcovers. Dean waited in the Land Rover with the engine running.

In the Indian shop, the village *duka*, we found a newly arrived shipment of imported Italian olive oil on the almost empty, dusty shelves.

Fantastic luck, a perfect gift. I bought one bottle for myself, one for Signora Manfriando, and Gemma bought out the rest of the shipment. Olive oil never appeared again on the shelves for the rest of our time in Mekele.

The *askiri* opened the factory gates for us when Dean honked, and we circled around the giant flame tree and parked. The carpenter and his assistant were busy in the yard, and the air smelled of cut wood. They must have worked late into the night, because there were now upturned tables on the ground in different stages of completion. The same camel from yesterday nibbled at sparse patches of dry grass. Old tools lay on the ground, and a pair of rough sawhorses had been set up by the front door.

"Every piece of wood's been cut by hand," Dean said. "No power tools, no precut wood from a lumber yard."

He unloaded two jerry cans of purified water from the back of the Land Rover and offered some to the carpenters.

"Annie, you'll need some basic Amharic, starting today. This in here," he said, pointing to the containers, "is *weha*."

He spent the next few minutes drilling me with difficult Amharic words and phrases, most of which I forgot as soon as I'd tried them out on my tongue.

"*Tena yastallann…*hello…*Tena yastallann…*" I practiced and repeated the odd words and pronunciations.

Dean had spoken to the local priests and to the tailors and shopkeepers in town the first two days we were in Mekele. He'd told them about the new factory and asked for help finding sewers and cutters, doing everything he could think of to spread the word. Now we sat on a rough, completed table, our legs dangling over the edge, and we waited. We had no idea what would happen, but we kept our eyes on the road from town, hoping someone would knock on the compound gates looking for work. We were open for business, but with no employees.

To stay busy and keep from worrying, Dean and I went inside to count the hides we had brought with us on the plane from Addis, while Gemma stood watch in the courtyard. We separated the calfskin from the heavier cowhides and the more exotic ones. We looked for damages in the leather and pulled those hides into a pile to be used for garments that took smaller pattern pieces, like vests. Then we separated them further by color and matched those with others of a similar shade—enough hides in each shade to make a pair of jeans, a jacket, or a vest—and we rolled them loosely together, separated those as ready to cut.

It was work I had observed many times in New York and I was confident with what I was doing. Dean caught on quickly, and we worked quietly and well together. The cool mountain morning warmed up. The tin roof absorbed the sun and the warehouse became uncomfortably hot. *By noon*, I thought, *it will be stifling in* here. I looked forward to the siesta hours ahead during the hottest part of the day and understood why it was a custom born from necessity.

"Dean, darling. Annie. Come quick! Look what's coming," Gemma called excitedly from the yard.

We dropped what we were doing and ran out to the yard, looking in the direction Gemma was pointing, speechless.

At first, all we could see was a cloud of dust on the dirt road leading from town. Kicking up that dust was a long, single-file trail of men, donkeys, and a few camels. The most unfortunate of the men had their antiquated treadle sewing machines strapped to their backs, like the livestock. It was an extraordinary scene, an ageless caravan. The men looked alike—tall and skeletal with gaunt faces, burnished skin, and unkempt, sparse beards. They were dressed alike, wrapped in their white cotton shawls like mummies, with tire-tread sandals on their dusty, callused feet.

We watched, weak-kneed with gratitude, as they made their way to the factory gates, burdened with their sewing machines, road dust covering their faces, legs, and white clothing. When they reached the courtyard, they unloaded their donkeys and camels and left them to graze among the outcroppings and along the compound walls. We met them in a receiving line in the shade beneath the flame tree, shaking hands, bowing in return to their bows, introducing ourselves and thanking them for coming. But it was they who were thankful—grateful for a weekly salary, money they could count on to feed their families.

"*Tena yastallann...*hello. *Weha? Weha? Weha?*"

We went from man to man, offering water from the jerry cans, pouring it into their cupped hands.

Gemma went around, writing their names in a ledger and having them sign in. Most were illiterate, signing an "X" where Gemma pointed, not even recognizing their own printed name. She had tried to get addresses and dates of birth, but she realized it was hopeless. A few men guessed at their ages.

They were there to work, and so the rest of the morning we spent moving the tables and sewing machines into the production lines I had envisioned. It got hotter in the factory as the morning went on. The stench was unbelievable—a hundred and fifty tanned animal hides, thirty unwashed men, and the sun beating down on the roof. What had been good for coffee bean storage provided almost impossible working conditions for a garment factory, but the tailors worked on without complaining, dragging the machines inches to the left or right, helping the carpenter outside, lining up the tables perfectly parallel with the walls under my direction.

I forgot about lunch with the Manfriandos until Matteo arrived, slowly navigating his green Citroën through the tailors' grazing donkeys and camels.

I met him in the courtyard, happy to see him walking across the dirt. The scene was one he was familiar with.

"*Buon giorno*, Anna, *buon giorno!*" he called out.

"Come see what we've done, Matteo."

He kissed me on both cheeks while Dean and Gemma watched curiously. He introduced himself to them, and, together, we walked the warehouse that was beginning to look like a small garment factory.

"*Meraviglioso…fantastico!*" he said, over and over again, although all he was looking at were nineteen antiquated sewing machines, three finished tables, and separated piles of leather hides.

"I can go to lunch?" I asked Dean. "The tailors can take lunch, too?"

"Of course," he said. "Do you need us to pick you up later?"

I looked at Matteo.

"No," he answered for me. "I'll bring her back here at four."

Dean nodded, poker-faced, and Gemma shot me a look, raising an eyebrow to her hairline. I slid in beside Matteo, and we drove away, small rocks and gravel crunching and spinning out beneath the tires.

Matteo drove across town, back up our mountain road, and stopped before olive-green metal double gates set into high walls topped with the same multi-colored glass shards I had seen at Dean and Gemma's home in Addis. He honked twice. One side of the gate swung open, pushed by a shriveled, toothless old man wrapped in a gray blanket who grinned happily and insanely, as if he hadn't seen Matteo in weeks instead of minutes. Matteo spoke to him in Amharic, and the old man pushed the other door open with all his weight against it. We passed through and drove up to the front door.

The Manfriandos' house was a single-story, unpainted, cinder-block structure set in the center of a dirt compound. There was an attempt at a lawn, but there wasn't enough water to keep it green and lush. On the right, there was a flourishing vegetable garden that got all the water and attention. Tomatoes grew in boxed cages as tall as I was. Green beans grew against teepee stakes. Vines covered every inch of earth in four raised beds, spilling over onto small pathways. I could see gorgeous eggplant, peppers of all colors, zucchini, and squash. Gourds and melons peeked from behind glossy leaves in the beds. It was glorious, the greens brilliant in the afternoon sun, the vegetables like colored jewels.

The Manfriandos were waiting for us when Matteo opened the front door into the living room. Signora Manfriando was short and heavy—a solid, straight torso from shoulders to hips—wearing an old-fashioned "I Love Lucy" fifties dress, with a white half-apron tied somewhere at her middle. She had an incredibly kind face, and I loved her instantly. She greeted me in enthusiastic Italian, took my face in her damp hands, and kissed my cheeks again and again. I gave her the olive oil, which pleased her, although I noticed later two large, imported, ten-liter tins in the kitchen.

And then there was Tino, Matteo's younger brother, smiling broadly, coming in from the garden with a full basket of tomatoes in different varieties, sizes, and colors. He was short and slim, dressed like Matteo in Levis, with masses of curly dark hair that stood out like a nimbus around his head and a Ringo Starr mustache too big for his face. He, too, kissed me repeatedly, after handing the basket of tomatoes to his mother. His English was as good as Matteo's, pleasing although heavily accented. He was warm and effusive, and, like Matteo, he had sad eyes.

Matteo was twenty-five and Tino twenty-three when I met them. They were as different in their looks as two brothers could possibly be, but they were best friends, imprinted and bonded for life.

Signore Manfriando stood behind his wife, tall and dignified, dressed in a white dress shirt, tie, and dark suit trousers. He kissed my hand in a courtly way without speaking a word. He maintained the same inscrutable expression throughout lunch, saying nothing directly to me, only nodding his approval of a dish from time to time. Neither he nor his wife spoke English, so it was up to Matteo and Tino to translate what we said. I brought out every Italian word I knew from my old Italian *Vogue* magazines and from every Italian menu or cookbook I had ever read.

Signora Manfriando indicated that we should come to the dining table in the front left corner of the sparsely furnished living room. It had been set with lovely, old-fashioned, hand-painted plates, ornate silverware, and starched white linens. Then she disappeared into the kitchen, and we settled into our chairs.

Signore Manfriando sat at the head of the table and poured the *vino rosso* (red wine). "Homemade," Matteo said. Signora Manfriando's place was at the foot, closest to the kitchen; Tino sat on his father's right; and Matteo sat on his left. A place for me had been set beside Matteo, to his left and Signora Manfriando's right.

The food arrived in waves, brought to the table by a young kitchen girl about the same age as Amira. There was minestrone soup and a basket of warm bread that smelled of oregano and Parmesan cheese, oil-cured black olives tossed with orange zest and fresh parsley, and marinated red and yellow peppers.

Next, Signora Manfriando came to the table with a deep bowl of handmade papardelle noodles with broccoli and garlic, and the kitchen girl followed her with a stack of pasta bowls.

After the pasta course, they brought in more serving dishes—thinly sliced chicken breasts baked with lemon, garlic, and capers and covered in rows of lemon slices; roasted potatoes with garlic and rosemary; green beans sautéed in garlic, olive oil and lemon juice; and thick tomato slices sprinkled with toasted bread crumbs and Parmesan cheese.

Dessert was a fruit bowl, and I watched the Manfriandos select, peel, and slice their choice with precision and artistry. Then there was coffee that had been roasted, ground, and pressed in the kitchen. Throughout the meal, Signora Manfriando basked in her husband's and sons' praise and pleasure.

"I hope your mother didn't go to all this trouble for me?" I asked Matteo, both dismayed and astounded at this extraordinary meal.

"No, Anna. This is no trouble. This is how she cooks every day for our family. On Sundays she cooks more because we have company then. But our supper, it is more simple…a salad, leftover soup, or pasta from lunch."

I was an American girl. Lunch in my world was a tuna salad sandwich, an apple, and a bag of chips, all eaten as quickly as possible. The Manfriandos sat at the table for an hour or more. They ate and drank, talked warmly and enthusiastically. They lingered over espresso and the last inch of wine in their glasses.

Back in New York, my family met for dinner at my grandmother's house on Sundays. She began cooking at seven in the morning to prepare everyone's favorite dishes, so there would be a chicken, a beef roast, a fish dish, always soup, three or four vegetables, and two or three desserts. I had cooked beside my grandmother since I was old enough to reach her kitchen counters with a step stool, so I had an appreciation for what had gone into the preparation of this meal at the Manfriandos. My grandmother cooked her extravaganzas once a week, but Signora Manfriando cooked like this for her family every day.

My grandmother and aunt shopped in a supermarket for those meals— the chickens, eggs, roasts, and vegetables all came packaged. Signora Manfriando grew her vegetables from seeds and chose them for picking when they were perfectly ripe; she killed, de-feathered, gutted, and cleaned the chicken in the back yard. She shopped only for flour, salt, pepper, and coffee beans in the marketplace. But she, my grandmother, and aunt all had the same secret ingredient—love. You know it when you taste it.

I helped to clear the table and tried to tackle the dishes, but Signora Manfriando shooed me away from the pile alongside the scratched and scuffed old-fashioned porcelain sink, pointing to the kitchen girl standing quietly in the corner. Matteo came into the kitchen and asked if I would like to take the *reposo* at his house.

I had just been treated to the most delicious meal of my life and now I was being offered a nap. I agreed to stay, sure I'd be shown a guestroom. Instead, Matteo took me by the hand to his bedroom and the big, carved wood bed he shared with his brother. Tino followed us in and sat down on the far side of the bed. I had never shared a bed with anyone else before.

The brothers kicked off their shoes; I did the same. They unbuttoned their waistbands; so did I. The three of us lay down, me on the far right, Tino on the far left, with Matteo in the center. Tino turned on his side, facing the wall and away from us, and fell asleep immediately. Matteo turned to face me and threw his top leg and arm over my torso. I leaned over to kiss him, and he whispered, "*Non qui, non ora*...not here, not now." And he, too, fell right to sleep.

It kept me awake for the next two hours, thinking how presumptuous Matteo had been and how I'd been rebuffed. The brothers snored softly, gone to me.

It would take me weeks to learn to nap in the afternoon. Americans don't nap. But I learned to appreciate that quiet time, even if I couldn't fall asleep quickly the way Matteo and Tino did. I loved to lie peacefully in bed during the hottest part of the day, listening to the birdsong outside, with the curtains drawn and stirring slightly in the breeze from an electric fan on the dresser, and the sunshine barely filtering through the windows.

Two hours later, the brothers opened their eyes at the same moment. We straightened our clothing and went back to join their parents at the dining table. Signora Manfriando had made a fresh pot of espresso and set out a plate with walnut biscotti for dunking.

No one said a word about the sleeping arrangements. Signora Manfriando invited me to lunch the next day, and then the next, and then to Sunday lunch with family friends, and it became a given—Matteo would pick me up at the factory at noon and bring me home for lunch every day.

I enjoyed helping Signora Manfriando finish the meal and bring it to the table. I ate beside Matteo and then we would take our *reposo* together with Tino sound asleep and oblivious beside us. Matteo and I touched and kissed each other, stealthily at first, and then more brazenly. Tino never woke.

The Manfriandos became my family. I became the Manfriandos' daughter, Tino's sister, and Matteo's girlfriend. I slipped into the role without even trying. The glass slipper fit.

# 8/ The Manfriandos: Mekele, Ethiopia

I have come across some black and white photographs of Matteo, his father, and some family friends standing in their garden. He must have been weeding in the sun before the picture was taken, because his outfit is so peculiar and so unlike him. He is wearing a white towel or pillowcase on his head, secured with a belt across his forehead, Arab style; large, dark sunglasses blocking his eyes; a week-old beard; a white dress shirt tied at the waist in a knot like a girl; and white briefs with the leg elastics stretched out, leaving nothing to the imagination. He looks like a half-dressed, Arab sheik who's forgotten his trousers. Only an Italian man would willingly and so proudly pose for a photograph in bright daylight in baggy underwear.

In another, Tino kneels in the yard beside his mother, hugging the little daughter of their housemaid, who's holding a homemade baby doll. His curly hair stands away from his face like he's been struck by lightning. Signora Manfriando is tiny beside Tino, almost as wide as she is tall, her gray hair pulled back into a severe bun, an apron tied around her non-existent waist. The photograph captures the love and pride she feels for her family, and Tino's love for his mother.

I was adopted into the family like a daughter-in-law and welcomed into the kitchen to cook beside Signora Manfriando. I attended the best cooking school in the world in her kitchen and in her vegetable and herb gardens. She spoke no English and I spoke only a small amount of Italian, but we communicated very easily with each other through gestures, lots of nodding, smiles, nouns, and poorly conjugated verbs. She knew I made her son happy and that I was comfortable in the kitchen with her. That was enough for her to teach me everything she knew.

It wasn't just that Signora Manfriando's food tasted so good, but how deft she was in the kitchen. Her knife skills were extraordinary. She sliced onions and garlic so thin they were transparent and she barely looked down when she sliced, cut, or chopped. She measured accurately by eye or feel, and her fingers seemed to know what to do without instruction from her brain. Her timing was meticulous—every dish ready at the right moment and served at the perfect temperature.

Nothing was ever thrown away. Onion and garlic skins, green bean stems, carrot tops, and potato peels became stock for the next day's soup; day-old bread and grated Parmesan cheese became garlicky, cheesy, herby breadcrumbs for a vegetable topping or a stuffing; leftover meats went into the next day's pasta sauce.

For my twenty-first birthday, Signora Manfriando made me an inventive birthday cake, using what she had to create perfection. She mixed crushed Uneeda biscuits from the Indian *duka* with sugar, cold espresso, chopped walnuts, melted butter, and cocoa powder, then rolled it into a log and poured chocolate ganache over the top. The butter hardened as it cooled, and it turned into a chocolate cake/candy bar—no baking necessary. I've tried to reproduce it a few times using different measurements of sugar, coco powder, and butter, but it never comes out the same.

That cake was one of many valuable lessons I learned in the Manfriando kitchen—how to use what I have and make something wonderful from nothing. Signora Manfriando didn't have a juicer, a blender, a waffle-maker, an electric pasta machine, or a coffeemaker. Her oven was a tin box that sat on a burner on her stove. She didn't even have a refrigerator. If she had butter, cream, or eggs she wanted to save overnight, she stored them outside on the shady kitchen windowsill. And she still turned out amazing meals, everything fresh, every morning.

I learned how to form potato gnocchi with the tines of a fork, how to knead and shape dough for long loaves of Italian bread, and how to make a true ragu tomato sauce with finely minced beef, carrots, onions, garlic, and cream.

We made pasta almost every day—dozens of shapes, dried, fresh, and filled. There was even one where we simply pressed the pasta dough through the holes in a colander into a pot of boiling water.

Under her wary supervision, I mastered the art of perfect pasta dough. I made a well in the center of a mound of semolina and all-purpose flour on the kitchen table, broke three eggs from her chickens into the center, poked each brilliant, orange yoke with a finger, added a splash of water, and quickly mixed it from the center outwards to form a ball of pasta dough. Signora Manfriando would guide my hands, mixing the dry flour into the wet so I wouldn't lose too much flour to the floor. When it was all incorporated into a smooth, elastic ball of dough, she would nod and give me an approving smile.

We would cut it into pieces and roll it through her hand-cranked pasta machine that she screwed to the edge of the kitchen counter, turning out sheets of pasta for nutmeg-scented spinach raviolis or lasagna, and cut linguini and fettuccine.

I'd bring the light-as-air spinach raviolis to the table with Signora Manfriando standing proudly behind me. She couldn't have been prouder if I had presented Matteo's first-born son.

I could read her mind perfectly, even though my Italian was just starting to come along.

"This American girl...*questo Americana feminile*...wants to learn. If my son marries her, at least he will eat well."

I especially loved Sundays when the factory was closed and I could work all morning beside Signora Manfriando to prepare a midday meal for her company. All the Italian expats and *ferenji*s in Mekele wanted an invitation to Sunday lunch at the Manfriandos.

She and I started at nine o' clock in the morning and produced six to eight exquisite dishes, plus bread or rolls and dessert, by noon. Tino or Matteo would bring in whatever was ripe from the garden, and Signora Manfriando would think for a moment and decide on the menu. Then she would send the boys back to the garden for herbs and garlic.

We fried eggplant rounds in a light, soupy batter, and sautéed broccoli with thin–sliced garlic, or spinach with raisins and minced onions. We mounded mashed potatoes around mozzarella cubes, rolled them in breadcrumbs, and fried them into croquettes.

We assembled deep vegetable lasagna casseroles, or tossed spaghetti with cream, eggs, grated Parmigiano Reggiano, fresh peas, and diced pancetta. I washed and tore—never cut—romaine lettuce leaves, radicchio, endive, sliced baby radishes, and orange segments for a refreshing salad tossed in olive oil and orange juice.

We baked small dinner rolls, twisted into knots and rolled in herbs, garlic, and melted butter. There was Signore Manfriando's good *vino rosso*, strong espresso served in heirloom demitasse cups brought from Rome thirty years ago, and a final shot of grappa to wash it all down.

Lunch lasted for three or four hours, and, finally, the guests groaned and pushed themselves away from the table. They strolled through the garden with Signore Manfriando or the boys to see what was growing, shared gardening advice, and smoked cigarettes. Then they would kiss goodbye, left cheek, right cheek, say their *grazie*s and *arrivederci*s, drive the short distance home, and take to their beds for a late *reposo* and Sunday afternoon sex.

If you had been blindfolded and dropped at the Manfriando table on a Sunday afternoon from somewhere else in the world, you would have sworn you were in Rome. But we were in Africa, and so much the better.

# 9/ Salt: The Danakil Depression, Northern Ethiopia

True to her promise, Lela invited me to dinner in the hotel dining room about a week after I settled into the *tukol*. Her only guest was a photographer/writer on assignment for *National Geographic Magazine* to produce an article on salt. I joined him at Lela and Rakesh's family table and sat across from him as he described the reason for his trip to Ethiopia.

"One morning at breakfast, shaking the salt over my scrambled eggs, I wondered where salt comes from; I just was curious and I wanted to find out. Salt's one of those things we never think about until we need it and don't have it."

He researched and discovered Ethiopia's Danakil Depression, only seventy-five miles and two hours east of Mekele, where most of East Africa's table salt is mined.

"It's one of the lowest spots on earth, much of it below sea level, with twenty-five percent of the world's active volcanos, flowing lava, bubbling hot springs, and underground lakes just beneath the surface salt crust; a fascinating, beautiful landscape…like I imagine the moon. Oh, and it's also the hottest place on the planet—average afternoon highs of a hundred and one degrees Fahrenheit…it could be a hundred and twenty or even a hundred and forty this time of year. I was even more curious once I read about the landscape, so here I am."

*He's used "curious" again*, I thought. *Some people are more curious than others. Maybe that's what makes them look outward into the world for their answers, while the less curious look inward.*

His name was Peter and he was the first true adventurer I'd ever met, looking exactly like I imagined a *National Geographic* photographer to look—older and graying, but fit, tall, tough, and friendly, dressed in khakis and camping boots and the photographer's many-pocketed khaki vest. He talked with Lela and Rakesh at the table, discussing travel routes, supplies he'd need, and possible guides from the Afar tribe in town. Rakesh warned him about the armed *shiftas* prowling the Danakil area that bordered the disputed Eritrean territory.

"Annie," Peter said suddenly, turning to me. "Would you like to come with me tomorrow, just for the day? Tomorrow's a scouting day and I could use the company."

The next day would be a Saturday, a half day at the factory. Although we had just got up and running, I knew Dean and Gemma would be fine with me taking off the morning for such an adventure. Matteo might feel differently, but this was something I wanted very much to do. I was a curious person, too.

"I would love to," I said quickly, grateful for the offer.

I sent a note with one of the waiters to Dean and Gemma's and another to Matteo and his parents, who would be expecting me for lunch the next day, and went out to the *tukol* to load up a small duffle bag. Our plan was to meet again at 4:00 a.m. the next morning in the lobby. Instead we met a half hour later upstairs by the guests' shared bathroom, bath towels over our shoulders, soap and toothbrushes in our hands.

"Traffic jam. You go first," he said courteously, making a small bow in my direction.

"No, you," I said. "You're the paying guest."

"You, Annie, please, I insist."

And so I did. I bathed quickly with the handheld sprayer, washing my hair and brushing my teeth as fast as I could, but still enjoying the hot water.

He was waiting by the door, leaning back against a wall, arms crossed, when I reappeared.

"Any hot water left?" he asked. But he was smiling.

"Plenty," I assured him. "This is the best hotel in Mekele...maybe the only one with hot water."

"It's the best in a two-hundred-mile radius," he said. "Believe me, I checked."

"Goodnight, then." Standing there with my dripping hair, in a cotton robe and flip flops, I could think of nothing more to say.

"Sleep well. See you at four," he said.

I scurried down the stairs and out to the *tukol*, shivering in the dark, the stone fortress/hotel looming above me.

A few hours later, at precisely 4:00 a.m., as I ran from the *tukol* to the hotel, I saw an unfamiliar Land Rover idling in the turn-around. Beside it was a tall, gaunt man in a ragged, baggy T-shirt, a dark plaid sarong, and a bandolier with bullets across his chest. A grenade belt hung from his narrow hips with a long, curved-blade knife like a small scythe tucked in at his waist. He leaned nonchalantly against the driver's side door with an automatic rifle over his shoulders; a frightening figure in the predawn dark.

Peter was waiting for me at the bottom of the lobby stairs, his camera bag, a large Ethiopian straw provisions basket, and a five-gallon yellow plastic jug of water at his feet.

"Good!" he exclaimed when I pushed open the front doors. "Here you are...good girl...right on time. We need to get there before sunrise. It'll be hotter than hell out there once the sun comes up."

"I think there's a driver waiting for us outside," I said. "He's pretty scary for a guide...more like an armed guard...or a *shifta*."

"That's the point. Rakesh told me he's the best in town. His name's Omar and he's an Afar—the scariest, most violent tribe in Ethiopia. There are Afar tribes from Ethiopia, Sudan, Eritrea, and Djibouti in the Danakil, all fighting over rights to the area...the rights to the salt mines. It's very dangerous on the roads right now, and the civil war is going on in the area as well. These Afar guys will behead a person or cut off a man's genitalia with their knives if they don't like the look of him. Omar is exactly what we need."

"I don't have male genitalia, but I do have a head, so maybe I should be worried," I joked unsteadily. Would I have jumped so quickly to join him if I had truly understood the dangers the night before? Two weeks earlier I wouldn't have known the answer to that question, but I did now; yes...a great big yes. What I'd already learned in Ethiopia was to say "yes" to everything placed in front of me, to go through every door that opened.

It was too early to make conversation as we took the east road out of Mekele. Lela had sent us with a breakfast of toasted bread and butter, and coffee in two large thermos bottles. We ate ravenously as though we hadn't eaten dinner only hours before. I dozed off and on in the back seat, my head resting against the window, jolting awake each time my head bumped against the window in concert with the potholes and ruts in the unpaved road. Peter's guide spoke not a word the entire trip.

As the sun rose over the mountains in the background, we reached the small town of Berahile, the entrance into the Danakil Depression and the salt mine center of commerce. Camels, hundreds of camels, were tied together single file, nose to tail, into biblical caravans of differing lengths, milling and restless in the dry sand. Some caravans were already piled high with rough-cut slabs of dirty white salt the size and thickness of a briefcase, ready at dawn to trek east across the desert to Somalia.

The camels stood patiently while the salt slabs were measured and taxed. Some lay on the ground, their legs with their giant knees folded up beneath them. The sun was already strong, the temperature already burning hot, and the air was still and utterly devoid of moisture. Sound traveled so far we could hear the camels' ropes straining.

When we stopped to buy some Cokes, Omar stood to the side and greeted other Afar men, as dour and impenetrable as he was. Unlike the Coptic Christians from Mekele, the warring Afars from this region are nomadic Muslims, hardened men with skin like leather hides, dried out like everything else in this land, taciturn and proud.

Peter and I found the District Commissioner in his office, a small cinder-block, one-story building with only a ceiling fan circulating the dry, overheated air. Everything would depend on his permission for the photo shoot and Peter's presence over the next few days. Peter signed some papers and we were on our way before the ink could dry so the D.C. didn't have even a minute to change his mind.

I watched from the Land Rover with the air-conditioning running as Peter immediately began photographing the busy commerce of Berahile with Omar by his side. He took shot after shot with a Polaroid Land camera for instant images and information, and then with his Hasselblad and Nikons, using light meter and tripod. When he felt he had enough, he and Omar jumped back into the truck, the sweat already soaked through Peter's T-shirt. I handed them both towels. We headed out of town and down into the salt flats of the Danakil Depression.

I was struck dumb by the landscape, so foreign, exactly like Peter had said; like the surface of Mars or the moon. No vegetation anywhere. Crusts of white salt lay at our feet like shallow ocean eddies, dried in long ripples as far as we could see, baking in the sun, cracking and flaking beneath our feet as we stepped.

Men worked in the fields, carving blocks of salt out of the ground with shovels and picks while the camels waited for their load, patiently resigned. How did they live here, in this heat, working at such backbreaking labor? And then they traveled hundreds of miles on foot with the camel caravans loaded with salt blocks, back to Mekele and further west to Sudan and across the Sahara Desert or east to Mogadishu, Somalia, and the Red Sea. How did they do it? How did the Afars do it for their entire lives and their ancestors' lives before them, possibly for the last million years? The fossilized remains of *Lucy Australopithecus*, the earliest known humanoid, were found right here, dating over three million years old.

Along the edges of the flats, sulphurous hot springs had bubbled up from beneath the surface, forming dried pillows of crusted mineral deposits in Dayglo orange, white, and yellow against the white salt ground and the searing, scrubbed white sky. The colors were so bright and electric they hurt my eyes as the day wore on. Peter snapped shots with intense concentration, never complaining about the heat, studying the Polaroids, learning about the light and the correct settings on his cameras as he worked, ever more curious with each subject.

We stopped work for an early lunch—hard boiled eggs, bread, and fruit from the hotel basket—under the shade of a cotton sarong tied to the Land Rover's overhead storage bars and two posts our driver dug into the salt. We drank water from camping mugs, doused towels from the plastic jug for our necks. We each slept for an hour; me in the rear of the Land Rover on a very uncomfortable side bench, Peter on the other. Omar preferred outside, beneath the shade of our temporary awning in case there was a wisp of a hot breeze to catch. No air-conditioning. The truck absorbed the heat from the sun and from the salt flats beneath us. The only sounds came from the camels groaning, resisting, or the quick, sharp voices of the salt workers. We slept hard as soon as we laid our heads down on our damp, rolled-up towels.

When we woke, we drove on to visit a volcano Peter had researched; one of the world's only active volcanos below sea level. We looked down into the crater and marveled. At that moment, the volcano was quiet. Beneath us, below the surface crust of salt and many miles inland, was the Red Sea, which dried up in the heat before it could reach the surface. While Omar rested in the shade of the truck, I helped Peter, loading and unloading film in the cameras as he worked. He shot a hundred rolls of film that day—thirty-five-millimeter color slide film, before digital photography, when every roll of film, every frame, was precious.

When the sun suddenly dropped and the light was gone, we drove back to Mekele, utterly drained but happy. As Omar drove west, the Land Rover rose into the mountains and we felt the change in temperature. We opened the windows and let in a gorgeous wind that cooled us, dried our hair and clothes, and relaxed us.

Of course, I'd studied basic geology and abstractly knew there were extreme differences in our planet. Yet that day I had been given the chance to see a landscape unlike any other on earth, so scorched, so unforgiving, so beyond my comprehension that I'd had no idea there were places in our world the shapes of which I could not even imagine.

It had been a difficult day, physically; I had never been so hot or so thirsty. But I'd seen something magical, something few people got to see even in photographs. I'd watched an expert nature photographer work and I'd learned something about myself. I had stamina and I'd been willing.

"You did well today," Peter said from the front seat. I could no longer see him clearly; the night was black with only a sliver of moon for light and we passed not another car on the road the entire trip to Mekele.

It was the best compliment I'd ever received.

A photographer had been curious and then he'd been generous.

# 10/ The Factory: Mekele, Ethiopia

The leather factory was never a success. It was not for lack of trying, or lack of enthusiasm, or idealism. It took us a while to accept that it was just not going to work.

The tailors from town were skilled enough to run up the straight seams of the native tunics, simple dresses, trousers, and the shawls and *shammas* (white wraps) everyone wore, but the leather jeans, jackets, and vests we were trying to make needed a higher level of sewing experience. They had been taught to sew by their fathers, and it was traditionally men's work. Who was I to say their sewing wasn't good enough? When I was unhappy with their work, I was insulting their fathers and their grandfathers.

The plodding, foot-operated machines didn't make the job any easier, or the final product accurate and clean. German industrial sewing machines promised by Ras Mengeysha never arrived. They may have made a difference, but maybe not.

Ethiopian men were proud and chauvinistic. Women were necessary for cooking, cleaning, children, and, of course, sex. The tailors didn't like taking instructions from me, nor from the poor nun or the female safari guide in shorts and camping boots, nor from the tall blonde in her high riding boots and mini-skirts. We were oddities to them, *ferenji* women to be endured. When I tried to explain in a combination of English, Italian, and Amharic why a seam or a stitched pocket wasn't good enough, I could feel the men stiffen with anger and shame, and disappear into themselves, their faces hardened into masks.

The men assigned to sorting the hides had trouble catching natural flaws, or bundling matching colors together. The damages would not get noticed by the sorter, the bundler, the cutter, or the sewer, and a finished pair of jeans would make its way through the production line until it reached me, Quality Control, where I would catch the flaw—a hole the size of a dime in the front leg. The men took any attempt I made to inspect their work as a personal insult to their manhood, no matter how respectfully I phrased my instructions. It all came down to my being a woman.

Gemma and I had wanted to hire women as sorters, trimmers, and packers. They were good jobs for women; the men could be the cutters and sewers. Dean didn't think it was a good idea. He didn't even want to hire a woman to sweep the factory floor of scraps and threads or clean the outhouses. Men and women didn't work side by side as equals in Mekele, and we weren't going to change that. It was a matter of pride that the men could provide for their families. There were sure to be problems if we tried to change tradition.

After the first few weeks, when my high expectations became too much of an insult, some of the tailors left for good. They strapped their machines on their backs and took them back to the marketplace in Mekele. Others reported for work only when they wanted, daring me with their body language and sullen stares to reprimand them.

The leather was difficult to handle and sew. The special sewing machine needles for leather were like miniature three-sided knives that cut, leaving holes in the leather that were permanent. The needles dulled easily, making large holes at the seam join, but we had to carefully conserve the supply I'd brought with me from New York.

Once a mistake was made setting the zipper or the back pockets, the garment was damaged permanently. I couldn't have the pockets reset because the holes from the needle would show. Without the electric sewing machines promised by Ras Mengesha, the tailors continued to push the needles through the leather, using the foot pedal machines. They believed they were trying their hardest and doing their best, and perhaps they were. It was just that their best wasn't good enough.

Maybe I was the problem, my tentativeness and my lack of experience. Or maybe, had I been a man, the tailors would have behaved differently. Every day I got more and more discouraged, unable to earn the tailors' trust and willingness and unable to turn out enough acceptable product.

It was very frustrating to Dean, Gemma, and me to see the damaged garments piled higher than the first quality ones that could be shipped to America.

When I would sink, Dean would tell me to keep at it, we were doing as well as we could, but we both knew the ship was going down. We all desired the same thing—employment for the people of Mekele—but it looked like it wasn't going to happen the way we planned.

There was one thing we could do that would make a difference, and it was Gemma's idea. We could teach the tailors how to read and write. I would teach Amira, too. Her great wish, she had confided, was that she longed to go to school.

On a trip to Addis to meet with Ras Mengeysha, Dean purchased dozens of basic Amharic and English schoolbooks and a schoolroom chalkboard. We began classes after factory hours at the picnic table beneath the flame tree.

Gemma had been in Ethiopia for two and a half years with the British Peace Corps, teaching high school English. Her Amharic, while not as good as Dean's, was good enough to guide the tailors through the primary school workbooks, and her British accent made her sound professorial and in command. She taught at the blackboard while I helped the men individually where they sat at the picnic table in the shade. Then I went home to the *tukol* and taught the same lesson to Amira.

Gemma was a natural, confident teacher. She was accepted by the tailors in a way I never was. They sat, rapt, like very good children, following her lessons on the board. The mini-skirts didn't hurt either.

We studied English and Amharic together, first learning to write our names, then the alphabet, then recognizing pictures of animals and household items and copying their names on the guided dotted lines. We conjugated verbs, added the nouns and punctuation, and put short sentences together. We read aloud the English language newspapers that arrived in Mekele a week or a month late.

We may not have sent more than a hundred pairs of jeans and fringed vests a month to America, but our true accomplishment in Mekele was that eighteen men learned to read and write in Amharic and English. They were hungry for this; they never missed a class and sat at the picnic table after lunch to study and do homework rather than nap during their siesta hours. Ras Mengeysha may have wanted a garment factory, but he got eighteen subjects who could read a newspaper, sign their names, and think for themselves.

It wouldn't matter what Ras Mengeysha may have wanted, because, by the end of the year, he would be executed during the military coup that would kill hundreds of the royal family.

# 11/ Men: Mekele, Ethiopia

Matteo's father, Signore Manfriando, was a tall, bald, dignified, man in his sixties, who led with his belly, as hard and as round as a soccer ball. Every morning, he put on a much-laundered and threadbare, starched, white dress shirt; a shapeless, black business suit; and a thin, black tie. He'd been retired from his role as the emperor's personal accountant for a few years, but he still dressed carefully each morning, as if planning for a meeting in the royal palace. The only thing missing from his daily business attire in Addis was his brown leather, accountant's briefcase. It sat polished and dusted beside his desk in the corner of the living room. They were both ready if a request should ever come from Addis for a meeting with Haile Selassie.

Signore Manfriando rarely spoke, and when he did it was formally and with every expectation his words would be respected and obeyed. I never once saw him touch his wife, although she had been taking care of him for more than thirty years, but he always complimented the dishes she set down on the table and served to him first. He was a good, but stern, man, definitely the head of his family and the king of his cinder-block castle. His sons deferred to him in all things and knew never to defy his wishes.

Signore Manfriando frightened me. I could feel his eyes on me at the dinner table, and, when I turned in his direction and smiled, he nodded but did not smile back. He said nothing to me directly during the first week I came for lunch. He kissed me politely on both cheeks when I walked into the house with Matteo, and again when we left for the factory. I knew the greeting was customary and not a sign of any real affection. He watched as I helped Signora Manfriando bring the bowls of pasta and platters of vegetables and meat to the table. He observed Matteo's affectionate behavior toward me in the house—his hand on my waist, on my hip, a kiss on the cheek when I sat down beside Matteo at the table—and said nothing in my presence.

After a month of cooking, serving, and clearing our unhurried lunches and our long, silent siestas, as well as my improving Italian, there was change. As I left the Manfriandos to return to my afternoons at the factory, Signore Manfriando would take my chin in both his hands and look kindly into my eyes as he wished me a good afternoon and evening. He didn't say much more than *buon giorno* and *buona serra, Signorina*, but I knew I had passed some kind of test. He had watched me be respectful and helpful to his wife, and had seen how accommodating and gentle I was with his son. He had observed me long enough to accept that, even though I wasn't Italian, I was a possible wife for Matteo. I was happy to please him, but I was always a bit afraid of him, as were his sons, and I never truly warmed to him.

Matteo was very close to his younger brother, Tino. They were together almost every minute of the day and night. Both young men still lived at home and had slept beside each other every day of their lives. It seemed that neither Matteo nor Tino chafed against their tightly circumscribed lives. The whole "free love, hippie movement," the biggest social influence in my early life, had passed them by. They were both happy enough living with their parents as though they were still young boys. They worked long, hot hours in the vegetable garden and at the refugee camp. They ran errands for their parents and chauffeured them down to the main street in town on market days, or up to the hotel for a rare dinner there or to place a phone call to Addis Ababa or Rome.

Every afternoon Tino, Matteo, and I left the table together for the family's sacred two-hour *reposo*. Matteo touched my hand or caught my eye with a look in his, a look like a held breath, as a signal it was time to leave the table. I helped to clear the dishes and then thanked Signora and Signore Manfriando for the delicious meal without meeting their eyes. I wished them a good rest and, embarrassed, let Matteo lead me by the hand to the bedroom. Tino would follow, lie down on the far side of the bed, turn his back to us, and, from a lifetime of practice, fall asleep immediately…I thought…I was pretty sure.

Matteo's need for sex overcame his original reticence with me in the bed beside him. The fact that his brother was beside us faded away as we kissed and touched each other a little more every afternoon—lifting of T-shirts, unbuttoning of waistbands, hurriedly unzipping flies, sliding off jeans and shorts and underwear, holding our breath, being careful not to wake Tino under the same blanket. It was a more powerful experience than I had imagined, to see and feel the need in Matteo, like a boulder picking up speed as it rolled down a mountain, and to feel it in myself.

Sometimes Tino suddenly stopped snoring, rolling on his side toward us, still asleep. We would hold our breath. Matteo's fingers stopped whatever they were doing, frozen against the soft skin of my breasts or between my legs, and it was like an unbearable ache, until Tino rolled back to face the wall, and we exhaled.

Matteo knew I was a virgin, always asking in a hoarse whisper for permission to move further. I was willing, more than ready. I had been longing to experience sex since I was fifteen, believing with all my teenage heart that if I didn't have it soon, I would die. In the dorm rooms at college, I had listened to girls talk about having sex with their boyfriends, but,

74

although I had dressed the part of a free love hippie, I was still a child, and I knew it. When the other girls talked, what I mostly felt was fear.

Eventually we made love, attempting to be as quiet and as still as we could, most of the time not even removing all our clothes. Matteo covered me with the whole weight and length of his body to keep me still, no flailing arms or legs, no moans that might wake Tino. He kept me quiet with his hand over my mouth while he whispered Italian endearments and suggestions in my ear. Sometimes just the Italian words, his voice caught in his throat, his breath against my ear, and the perfect touch in just the right place, were enough to bring me to a squashed and suppressed orgasm.

When I had fantasized about sex before, I had imagined it to be more than these hidden gropes and touches, and certainly without a brother in the bed. We were having siesta sex, quiet sex, not the whole Broadway production. I had known next to nothing before Matteo, but I knew there had to be more to it than what was happening beneath the blankets.

The first time we had truly uninhibited, private sex, we were alone and away from the house. We were in his Citroën at sunset, waiting for the animals to come out to the watering hole in the canyon. We sat in the car in silence, holding hands across the gearshift box and watching as the animals came down to drink. After they had lapped cautiously at the stream and wandered off into the mountains in the fading light, Matteo reached across me and opened my car door.

"*Carina,*" he said. "Come with me."

We walked down to, and crossed over, the shallow stream and stood exactly where the animals had been drinking. Matteo pointed out the different hoof prints in the mud, showed me which marks belonged to which animal, and whose scat had been left behind. The smell of the animals lingering in the air was overpowering—musky, rank, and dense—like the elephant enclosure in a zoo. I was not just observing Africa from a distance, but standing right at its heart.

The scent and the miracle of the moment unleashed something in both of us. We looked at each other and just knew it was time. We had kissed, touched, and even come against each other enough under his blanket. Matteo took my hand and led the way through the rocks and dust, back to the car. He leaned me back against the hood, quickly unzipped, pulled down my shorts, and pushed inside me. I had been expecting it to hurt, but it didn't, and, with all the practice we had had, this final step felt inevitable and right.

We both came quickly and caught our breath against each other. The animal smells, the setting sun, the darkening sky above the mountain ridges, the music from the stream, the hyenas yipping to each other as they prepared for the night's hunt, made me feel like I was making love, not just to Matteo, but to Africa itself. It was my first time, and, although as a

75

fifteen-year-old I had fantasized about making love, I could never have imagined it happening like this.

"What does it feel like?" I asked Matteo. I had so much to learn.

"What do you mean? When I come?"

"No, to be inside me."

"It feels like coming home," he said. "It feels like where I'm supposed to be."

\*\*\*\*\*

My Italian language education began with words for food and food preparation, and then sex. I had to be careful when I was first learning, because I could easily mix up the two genres.

"*Lo amo le penne*," (I love your penne) was something I might say to Signora Manfriando as I took my first bite of that day's pasta dish.

"*Lo amo suo pene*," was very similar, and something I might say only to Matteo in bed.

"*Scopami cazzo me*." (Naughty word...Guess, or look it up!)

"*Baciami*." (Kiss me.)

"*Di tocare me qui*." (Touch me here.)

"*No se fermano*." (Don't stop.)

"*Carina*." (Sweetheart.)

"*Ti amo*." (I love you.)

And my favorite, "*Tesora*." (Treasure.)

Whether Matteo really meant it or not, just hearing the whispered words against my neck sent shivers through me.

Everything sounds sexy in Italian. Speak the following words out loud, nice and slow, and hit the accent hard on the first syllable (except for "*amore*," with the accent on the second syllable).

"*Il mio amore, fa la base, prego*." It sounds romantic, but it means, "My love, make the bed, please."

I learned from Matteo the many Italian words for love, affection, slang, sex acts, and dirty expressions at the same time we perfected the art of the silent and almost motionless orgasm, his parents sleeping on the other side of the wall and Tino softly snoring beside us.

What did his parents think was going on in that bedroom, day after day? I could not imagine. Perhaps they did know and it was an accepted European custom. Or they believed it was Matteo's due as the first-born son, to be fed like a king by his mother and made love to like a prince. And I played the part of the princess from a kingdom far, far away, the Cinderella of my childhood to an Italian Prince Charming with a three-day-old beard.

We only discussed one time that Matteo would never spend the entire night with me in my sleeping bag in my *tukol*. In his mind, it was okay for us to have sex right under his parents' noses every afternoon, but he needed to be home with his family most evenings and sleep in his own bed beside his brother.

The first time I asked him to sleep with me until morning, he was hopping from foot to foot by my sleeping bag, slipping into his jeans after a long evening entertaining each other with Broadway sex.

"They wait for me to come home, Anna. My mother makes fresh biscotti at night and, sometimes, pizza."

What could I say? I'd tasted Signora Manfriando's walnut biscotti dipped in chocolate and her pizza Margherita. I knew I couldn't hold a candle to that.

It was bewildering to me—a women's lib product of the sixties and seventies—but, as the girlfriend of a traditional Italian man, and brought up to always be respectful of the differences in others, I just accepted things the way they were. I didn't know if what we had between us was love, but I had a feeling that, if it really was, I would know it.

I'd never been anyone's girlfriend before. The Jane Goodall in me wanted to explore this new world in Africa. Cinderella just wanted to belong to someone.

# 12/ Famine: Mekele, Ethiopia

I cooked and ate at the Manfriandos like I never had before, but we were well aware of the famine in the province and the starving, wandering refugees lost outside our homes. They stopped at the Manfriandos' gates every day, searching for the camp, unable to take another step without water and food. Their *askiri* had instructions to open the gates to anyone in need, to offer water, to show them to the kitchen door for vegetables from the garden.

Dean, Gemma, and I were focused on the factory, but, most afternoons, Matteo and Tino took baskets of vegetables to the doctors in the refugee camp located in the far valley below our mountain on the other side of town. They volunteered beside Dr. Horst and his Ethiopian physician wife, Dr. Sofiya.

Matteo often asked me to volunteer at the camp with him, but all my time was spent building, worrying about, and shoring up the leather factory.

"There it is," Matteo said one evening when we sat behind my *tukol* at the edge of the cliff. He pointed to some open, flat land in a valley below us, mostly hidden by another mountain.

"That land next to the lake?" I asked, following where he was pointing.

If I squinted, I could make out strung tarpaulins, canvas tents, and domed huts thrown together with no obvious layout beside a small, almost black lake.

"That's not water, Anna," Matteo said. "It's a lake of *mierde*...a lake of shit."

The camp was run by Dr. Horst, a small, thin Bulgarian with sunburned skin and a sparse, unkempt, blond comb-over, and his graceful Ethiopian wife. Dr. Horst may have been slight and frail looking, but he had the determination of a general in the battle for his life.

They often came to the Manfriandos for Sunday lunch. Dr. Horst was often harried and distracted, but Dr. Sofiya knew it was important for her husband to take some time away from the relentless illness and death they lived with. Signora Manfriando fussed over him and made his favorite Italian dishes, and Dr. Sofiya coaxed him to eat more.

They rarely talked at the dinner table about what went on in the camp, but they always had up-to-date news and rumors about the Communist political demonstrations, the latest Royalist army officer defections, and the disappearances in the capital. They communicated with the medical community in Addis almost daily, and they were the most dependable source of news in isolated Mekele.

This was the tenth year of drought and the second year of a brutal famine that had begun in the Western Sahara-Desert nations and traveled east across Africa to Ethiopia. A temporary feeding station had been set up by the local government on a twenty-acre plot of land planned to temporarily house a thousand people. Families fleeing from the hardest hit provinces to the west quickly overwhelmed it. Dr. Horst estimated that five thousand people were living there permanently now. It quickly became what it really was—a refugee camp. With almost no help from the emperor, who was battling to hold onto his three-thousand-year-old dynasty, and very little international relief aid reaching Mekele, Dr. Horst, Dr. Sofiya, and their volunteers did the best they could.

They were also the only Western doctors in Mekele, splitting their time between their office, home visits, and the camp. They did everything from delivering babies, to pulling infected teeth, to removing tumors. They took care of all the *ferengis'* sore throats, birth control, and bouts of diarrhea, and dearly liked to be paid in cash. Most of their patients were Ethiopian peasants who had given up on the local medicine man or Coptic priest. They came to see the doctors with late-stage, serious diseases, paying only what they could afford—many times there were only a few eggs wrapped in their shawls.

Daisy and I went to Dr. Horst only once, for a case of protracted diarrhea. He examined us both without comment; he acted as the only veterinarian in Mekele as well. I paid him for the visit and the antibiotics. When I left, there were at least a dozen people waiting outside his office, propped against the wall with legs splayed, or squatting. None of them looked like they could pay for the doctors' services. I went back inside and emptied my change purse on the counter.

One Sunday, Dr. Horst confided to the Manfriandos that, the night before, he had dreamed there had been a polio outbreak in the camp. It was his worst fear.

The camp was woefully undersupplied, not nearly enough food, medicine, water, or latrines. Dr. Horst worried constantly about typhoid, cholera, and dysentery; he fought those infectious diseases like they were true foes, working around the clock, forty hours at a stretch with no sleep.

Another Sunday, he arrived late for lunch, distressed and heartbroken. He had lost a mother and two children that morning to advanced malnutrition, and had just left an inconsolable husband and two more children back in the camp. They had heard about the feeding station in Mekele, hundreds of miles from their village, and had survived their journey through the mountains, only to arrive too late to avoid this tragedy.

He was failing as a doctor, he told us at the table, his head in his hands, and close to tears. Failing. This man, this angel fighting famine, biblical diseases, and corruption, believed he was failing.

Sundays were my only days off from the factory, but, after hearing Dr. Horst talk about the mother and her children who had just died, I wanted to help. After lunch, rather than take our customary *reposo*, Matteo, Tino, and I followed the doctors in their battered Jeep down the mountain to the camp.

We entered through the front gates and drove through a slum of hastily constructed shelters made from cardboard, tarpaulins, fabric, sheets of plastic, corrugated tin, and tree branches. Plastic jugs and tin bowls lay scattered in the dirt. Children in tatters—filthy shorts and T-shirts with more holes and rips than fabric—came running after the doctors' Jeep and the Citroën, calling to us.

That lake I had seen from my *tukol* was, indeed, a lake of *mierde*. Herons pecked at grass growing along its edges like it was a real lake, but the smell was unmistakable.

"Matteo," I moaned, bringing my T-shirt neck up to my nose.

"In an hour you won't even notice it," he reassured me.

We parked in front of a large white tent with a red cross on the sides, the main medical tent. Matteo went off to organize a game of soccer with the older, stronger boys, Tino went to the surgery tent to assist in the makeshift ICU, and Dr. Sofiya put me to work with her.

There was a long line of shell-shocked men, women, and children waiting patiently outside the tent—new arrivals, Dr. Sofiya said. I was to walk among them, looking for children in peril. They were the ones most at risk of dying from malnutrition and they needed to be seen as soon as possible. I was to measure the width of the children's upper arms with a red ribbon marked with different widths for different approximate ages, and, if they were less than the lengths marked, I was to bring those children and their families to the front of the line.

These were devastated people, walking skeletons who had reached the limits of their strength. They had left everything they owned in the hope they could save their children from starvation, walking hundreds of miles and burying children and the elderly along their trek.

The newly arrived women didn't have the strength left to stand. They sat in the dirt, attempting to get a listless, glassy-eyed baby to suckle. Some of the children were so close to death, even to my untrained eyes, that there seemed little hope of saving them, but I rushed the babies and their mothers to the front of the line and called to Dr. Sofiya. She or one of her assistants came out to assess the situation and ushered them into the tent.

"Keep calm," an Ethiopian woman volunteer advised me in English.

But, witnessing the dying babies for the first time, it was difficult to keep the panic from my voice.

Toddlers with twig limbs, the skeletal faces of old men, and distended bellies, hid in their mother's dirty *shammas*. When I reached down to measure the children's arms, I met no resistance. Their arms were limp, little more than chicken bones, their eyes blank.

I worked, shocked by the grief around me, until the early evening, when Matteo tapped my shoulder and indicated we should go.

"We can't leave these people," I said.

"Yes, Anna, we can," he said firmly. "There is tomorrow and the day after that. There will be many more days and many more people."

"Right outside our doors, Matteo. It's a sea of misery. I feel terrible...I didn't understand...I didn't know."

"Yes, it is that—a sea of misery," Matteo said, shifting the gears too forcefully as we drove out of camp. "And the army requisitions the food aid that does arrive from the West and they sell it for weapons. Relief comes in on large transport planes, and the contents never make it further than Addis."

"Do you think the emperor knows this is happening in his country?"

"He knows, but he has other things he is worried about right now. The traitors and Communists are circling above him like vultures."

"I want to come back next Sunday, do what I can," I said. "I'm no good with blood and wounds and needles, but I can do other things to help."

"You did a good job this afternoon. Dr. Sofiya told me," Matteo smiled. "*Carina*, you'll be surprised what you can do."

He was right. In the months to come, I would feed hundreds of babies and toddlers from the stacked cans of formula, powdered milk, and jumbo jars of peanut butter. I held out plastic bowls so ICU patients could vomit or defecate. I washed baby bottles and old men who were more bones than flesh, with death already in their eyes. I held a woman's hand as she died, her baby tucked beside her in her cot. And, when Dr. Horst or Dr. Sofiya thought I needed a change from the medical tent, they sent me to the little school tent to teach letters, numbers, and songs to those children recovered enough; those who still remembered how to smile and laugh.

# 13/ Rain: Mekele, Ethiopia

After a decade of drought, the big rains finally came that year to the mountains in northern Ethiopia.

Massive gray clouds, the color of battered tin, formed slowly over the jagged mountain peaks during the mornings and darkened the sky by noon day after day. Pushed by the wind, heralded by thunder that rattled the tin roof, and sounding like those roofs were being lifted and shaken by a giant, we watched the cloud masses build and hoped they were headed our way.

The entire town hoped and prayed that this year the rains would really come. Dean and Gemma, Amira, the Manfriandos, Dr. Horst, the tailors, the Indian who ran the general store, the hotel waiters and kitchen staff—everyone I knew—studied the storm clouds, discussed them over meals and when we met each other in town.

For weeks, we watched as the clouds built, but we were disappointed day after day as the wind shifted direction, or the clouds dissipated, and our hope for rain disappeared with them. It was July, what should have been the middle of the big rains season and Ethiopia's winter, and all we had seen were those heavy clouds, the thunder that made our teeth ache, lightning slicing across the sky, and a crackling electricity in the air.

But, one afternoon, the ominous cloudbank finally released its promise. Matteo pointed out the edges of the rainstorm, defined in the sky like in a pencil sketch, and we watched the wind blow the downpour into graceful curving sheets as it fell to earth. From our mountain roost, we could make out where the storm began and where it ended, carrying lightning and thunder along in its path. It wasn't far off and it looked like it was moving in our direction.

When the squall arrived, frightening in its ferocity, it tore down what little electricity service there was and washed away tarmac and dirt roads alike, turning them into sudden, raging rivers that took branches and rocks, small mammals and snakes tumbling downhill in its wake. The rain came down in sheets that swamped the windshield wipers of our vehicles and poured with such force that mud huts disintegrated, sections of corrugated tin were ripped from roofs, and lorries lay overturned and discarded, their cargo spilled and spoiled on the roads.

The smudged gray cloud-cover hung oppressively over our town for weeks, building every morning and then letting loose torrents of rain in the afternoon. We had wished for this, prayed for this, but, when it came, we were miserable. At our elevation, the clouds felt like they were pressing down on our heads. The temperature at dawn was in the low forties and nudged toward the fifties by midday. We were always cold and always wet.

Our discomfort was nothing compared to that of the local people. They owned only the lightweight shawls they wore all year long and, if they were fortunate, rubber tire-tread sandals. They lived in small mud huts and walked tens of miles up and down the mountain paths each day, soaked through to the skin, as mud splashed across their legs and the hems of their wind-whipped, white clothing.

Amira moved in with me to save herself the trip home each day. Now confined to the hut all afternoon with even less chores to do, she walked down to the Manfriandos to help the Signora with lunch. The tailors arrived for work before dawn, soaked and shivering under useless umbrellas with broken spokes. Production was able to continue without electricity because we were still sewing on the ancient pedal machines.

Daisy and Negiste huddled miserably under the porch eaves between the leaks. My straw ceiling leaked, too, and, when I flattened my palms against the whitewashed mud walls, I could feel that they were damp. My sleeping bag and towel were always cold and clammy.

The Manfriandos' home was made from cinderblocks with a corrugated tin roof, and, when the rain fell, it sounded like automatic weapon fire ricocheting off the ceiling. We shouted to each other over the racket in the kitchen and across the table. We put old paraffin tin cans on the floor to catch the drips from the patches and the rusted-through spots in the roof. The clatter from the drops hitting the tins was a counterpoint to the clamor from above.

Signora Manfriando cooked heavy bean and meat soups and baked pasta dishes to warm her family and lift our spirits. She and Signore Manfriando wore threadbare, shapeless, wool cardigans in the house—hers over her housedress, and his over his vest and under his suit jacket.

During siestas, I was unable to sleep, although Matteo and Tino slept well, oblivious to the cold and the noise. I lay on my side with my knees pulled up to my chin, Matteo on his side behind me, his arm wrapped around me. I shivered under the layers of blankets, unable to get truly warm, even pressed against the full length of Matteo's body.

I listened to the cacophony on the roof and watched the drips land, one by one, in the tin on the floor by my side of the bed. The walls of the bedroom were painted a pale yellow, and the window was covered with yellow cotton curtains. Normally when I woke in the late afternoon, the room glowed from the waning sunlight filtering through the fabric. Now the room was in shadows and as gray as everything else in Mekele. The cold and the dampness were inside me, inside all of us. I could not shake a feeling of abandonment. It felt like the rest of the world had left us to fend for ourselves on this rain-soaked, shrouded mountain in northern Africa.

Only Gemma owned proper clothing for the weather. She had a London-worthy assortment of sweaters, matching wool skirts, thick, colored tights, and bright yellow rubber rain boots...even a heavy-duty, intact golf umbrella.

The cuffs of my wool socks and my camping boots were wet all day and never completely dry by morning. I shopped for warm clothing at the Indian *duka* but found only scratchy, men's jeans and cheap, polyester sweaters in fluorescent hot pink and lime. Instead, Matteo gave me a pair of his soft and faded Levis and a long-sleeved, thermal undershirt, and I wore them every day, although now the back legs of my jeans were wet instead of my legs. Gemma lent me a gray cardigan and gave Amira a pullover that had shrunk in the wash and no longer fit.

The first day of the big rains, it rained hard all through our siesta. Dean and Gemma came to pick me up as usual at four o'clock for another three or four hours of work.

"Don't go," Matteo said, waking to the sound of Dean's insistent honking outside the Manfriandos' gates, pulling me back to the mattress. In the dark, he had overslept. "It's not safe to go out in this rain."

"I have to go," I said. "They're here. The tailors are waiting for me at the factory." I released his hand from my arm.

"Let me talk to Dean, then," he said, throwing back the covers and slipping into his jeans. "He won't know how to drive these roads in the rain."

He snapped open a gray plastic tarpaulin by the front door and held it up for us to use as protection from the rain as we ran to the gates. The Manfriandos' day guard slid them open for us. He was the picture of wretchedness—muddy legs and bare feet, and a sodden, dripping blanket over his head, clasped under his chin.

"Do you want me to drive you down the mountain and pick you up later?" Matteo shouted over the rain to Dean, leaning into the driver's-side window with the tarpaulin over his head.

"I'll be fine driving," Dean answered. "It rains in Chicago, too."

"Have you driven a Land Rover in water up to your fenders on a mountain road in Chicago?" Matteo asked, undeterred by Dean's dismissal.

"That won't happen."

But that is exactly what happened.

On our way down the mountain, we got swept up in a deluge that overtook us on our narrow, dirt road. For a moment, we lost traction and I felt the Land Rover lifted and carried by the water. We hit something that stopped us with a jolt, and I heard the scraping sound of metal as we crashed into a boulder the size of an armchair that had not been in the middle of the road on our way up to lunch earlier. We were wedged in place. And, indeed, the water rushed around us, at times as high as the side fenders, and seeped in through the supposedly watertight doors.

"Should we open the doors and make a run for it?" Dean asked, very frightened.

"That can't be right," I said. I had no idea what we should do, but jumping into rushing water carrying tree branches, rocks, and parts of people's homes in its wake down a mountainside couldn't be the right choice.

*What would Matteo say? What would my father say?* I tried not to panic. *Trust the Land Rover to do its* job, I thought. *That's what my father would say. It must be the most-used vehicle in Africa for a reason.*

Gemma sat frozen solid and mute in the front passenger seat, watching the water pouring in around her yellow rain boots.

We waited out the storm—it lasted not more than half an hour, but it felt like much more—worried every moment that the mud and water pouring under and around the tires would cause the boulder holding us fast to the mountain to give way.

"This can't be happening," I said over and over again, knowing I was completely powerless. Every time something new smashed against the truck, I held my breath, my heart thudded, and I waited for the Land Rover to wrench itself free and float off the road and over the cliff.

When the rain slowed, and the flash flood subsided, we walked back through the muck to the Manfriandos' for help. Matteo, Tino, the day guard, and the gardener came back with Dean and, together, they lifted the Land Rover's front end and released it from the boulder. There were new scrapes along the undercarriage, and the front bumper was dented. The damage was negligible, just the latest in a long history of mishaps and near misses. The front axle was fine, and we continued down the mountain to the factory.

Matteo said nothing at all to Dean as he worked to release the vehicle, but he spoke to me later that evening when he picked me up in his Peugeot. We drove through the town and the surrounding roads. Mekele, always on the verge of disintegration, had been devastated by the violent storm. The ground had been so desiccated that it had absorbed the deluge almost completely, leaving only great, muddy fissures in the landscape.

On the drive up the mountain, I noticed the sides of our road had washed away in big sections, leaving it even narrower, and the landmarks we knew by now and could negotiate in the dark—the rocks and potholes and cracks in the road—had rearranged themselves into a new obstacle course.

"You could have gone over the side of the mountain," Matteo said, looking straight ahead as he drove.

"I know that now," I said.

"You were lucky today, Anna."

"I know."

"I want to take you back and forth to the factory during the rains," he insisted. "You have to listen to me, Anna. If I tell you it's too dangerous to drive down the mountain, it is not because I want you to spend the afternoon in bed with me."

"Okay, okay..."

"Anna, don't dismiss me."

"I'm not...I won't," I promised, backpedaling, flustered. We both knew that I *had* dismissed him earlier. I *had* shaken off his hand and his warning.

He dropped me off at my home and did not come back that night. I had plenty of time to think about it, lying alone in my sleeping bag in the dark and listening to the leaks trickling through the sodden straw into tin cans Amira had placed around the room. Yes, I had dismissed his advice, and now there was a bigger question I needed to think about. Did I really respect Matteo? Even at twenty-one, I knew there was no real love without respect.

The next day, the clouds massed early and the rain came in the morning. Through our lunch and siesta, a pale sun asserted itself. Dean and Gemma pulled up to the Manfriandos' at four o'clock and honked again for me. Matteo pushed himself up against the headboard, crossed his arms across his chest, looked at me and didn't say a word. Would I go with Dean and Gemma or wait for him?

"I forgot to tell Dean not to pick me up," I said lamely, combing my hair into a ponytail with my fingers and tucking the thermal shirt into my jeans as I dressed. "And it's not raining."

"No, it's not," he said, agreeing, and accepting something about me in that moment. "But I'm here if you need me."

The thunderstorm between us passed.

I reached below the bed and felt for my damp socks and boots. "Can I borrow a pair of dry socks?"

"Only if you let me see your breasts again before you leave," he said, smiling for the first time in two days.

I took a pair of socks from a drawer, slipped them on, tied my shoelaces, and lifted my shirt to my neck for him as I backed out of the bedroom door.

On the way to the factory, a hailstorm let loose, all the more freakish with the sun shining weakly in the sky. We were bombarded by hail the size of lemons and oranges—compacted balls of ice, heavier and much more dangerous than snowballs. Dean pulled over to the side of the road, and we sat in a vehicle built strong enough to withstand a charging rhino attack while ice balls smacked into the roof, the doors, and the windshield.

None of us had ever seen anything like it. We waited it out—it lasted only a few minutes—our hearts racing hard for the second time in two days. Then we circled the Land Rover and checked for damage. The roof was pockmarked, there were new dents in the doors, and the windshield now had spidery cracks.

"We need to get to the factory right away," I said, no longer fearful for myself, but worried for our workers. During their lunch breaks, the tailors usually ate something, then napped or studied their English lessons under the shelter of a big tree in the compound. They might have walked the few miles to town and back, to work for a few hours in their own tailor shops. Some of them would have certainly been on the road and exposed to the force of the hail.

When we pulled into the factory gates, one of the tailors was lying on the ground and others were milling around him. Conscious but dazed, he held to his head a rag soaked in cleaning fluid that we used to spot-clean finished leather garments. Gemma got to him first, lifted the rag away, and saw that he was bleeding from a large abrasion on the left side of his face and forehead.

"Do you want me to go for Dr. Horst?" I asked. An image crossed my mind of the thousands of refugees milling about the open field of the feeding station. What had happened there during the storm?

"No, I think he'll be okay if we replace this cloth with a clean one and let him rest for a while," Gemma answered, sinking to the ground and cradling the tailor's head in her lap.

It occurred to me that I had underestimated Gemma, as well as I had Matteo. Just when I dismissed her in her matching wool outfits and rain boots, she took a bleeding man into her arms with no concern for herself or her cashmere sweater.

Another tailor had been hit by hail as he walked unprotected from town, and showed up late to work with big welts on his face and shoulders. A young shepherd boy and two of his sheep had been killed in the field next to the factory. Without even a single tree near them, the boy had been unable to find shelter for his flock in time when the storm hit.

Matteo picked me up at seven o'clock, subdued. He and Tino had spent the afternoon helping Dr. Horst. Many of the refugees had been hurt, some badly, and three had died—a crippled old man who had only been able to crawl toward shelter, and a frail mother and her sick baby. "Will you come home with me now and have dinner tonight at my house?" he asked. "My mother is preparing a meal for the camp staff and I am going to take it to them after we eat. Come with me."

I thought misery was wet socks, cold feet, and a dripping roof. But I learned real misery is having no food to feed yourself or your children, no shelter, no warm clothes, a dying baby in your arms, then a rainstorm that soaks all the belongings you have in the world that you've carried to a camp two hundred miles from your home, and, the next day, you wake up in a first-aid tent with a concussion and bruises from a hailstorm you can't remember.

# 14/ Faith: Lalibela, Ethiopia

Matteo owned a motorcycle—a nail-polish-red and chrome Kawasaki muscle motorcycle. There was nothing sexier to me than seeing him astride his bike, his long legs in his American Levis, his eyes shaded in dark sunglasses, wearing a perfectly pressed white dress shirt courtesy of Signora Manfriando and her heated charcoal iron.

Every workday the sun shone, he'd be waiting for me outside the factory compound at noon, leaning patiently against the parked bike, legs crossed and stretched out in front of him. Bathed, shaved, and tanned after a morning under the sun in the Manfriandos' garden or the refugee camp, he smelled deliciously of soap, starched cotton, and a citrusy, Italian aftershave. He'd raise his sunglasses to his eyebrows and nod with a slight upward movement of his freshly razored chin. In front of the blank and inscrutable faces of the Ethiopian tailors there was no hug, no kiss, or even a spoken hello. In public, Matteo was as taciturn and undemonstrative as his father.

"Are you hungry?" Those were the first words I heard from him every single day.

This particular day was a Friday. It was the start of an Orthodox Christian religious holiday. We were closing for the rest of the weekend, and it was my first full weekend away from the factory.

"Are you hungry?" Matteo asked again.

"Oh, yes, I'm hungry," I grinned. "I'm always hungry."

"Let's take a trip this weekend with the motorcycle...*con la motocicletta*," he said. "I want to show you someplace great."

"Yes! Anywhere. I'm dying to see more of Ethiopia."

I was hungry for more than lunch. I'd been training the tailors for two weeks, working long days, coming home each night more and more discouraged with our lack of progress, and had seen nothing of the country other than the Mekele market, the factory, the hotel, the inside of the Peugeot, and visits to Matteo's animal watering hole.

Over lunch at the Manfriandos', Matteo told me about the ancient religious city of Lalibela. Ethiopia is one of the oldest Christian countries in the world, and Lalibela was built as a monastery in the early days of Christianity. A group of small churches, hand-carved out of the surrounding mountains two thousand years before, remain intact and are protected as a World Heritage Site. 'Marvels of Faith,' Matteo called them.

"It sounds great," I said. "How long a drive is it on the motorcycle?"

"*Non c'e problema*," Matteo said, running his hand back and forth across his smooth right cheek and jaw—a sure sign to me that he had some reservations. I'd seen it before. "Three hours…at the most."

"Where will we sleep?"

"I remember a small *pensione* I stayed at once before and I'm sure I can find it again, but, tomorrow, with the holiday, the town will be full and it will be difficult to find a room. We will need our sleeping bags…a tent… some water…and some food as a *precauzione*."

This was getting more complicated and even dangerous. How would we balance our housing and our meals on the back of a motorcycle?

"Are you sure you don't want to take the car?"

"No, *carina*," he said. "Let's have an *avventura*."

"When do you want to leave?"

"Let's go right after lunch. I'll take you home first, supply the bike, and come back for you. Drink water now. Change to jeans and a T-shirt with long sleeves. Wear a hat. We'll be in the sun all afternoon." He barked instructions and sounded just like his father.

*I hope he can take care of me*, I thought, thinking like my mother.

Now that it was a definite plan, we finished lunch quickly. Signora Manfriando went back to the kitchen and began to cook a weekend's worth of meals for us, Tino went off for his *reposo* without us, and Matteo drove me home so I could throw some clothes in a duffle bag. Amira agreed to stay in the *tukol* with Daisy and Negiste.

An hour later, Matteo came roaring up to the hut with the rear bumper of the bike piled high with our supplies strapped tightly together. It reached above Matteo's full height in his seat. I lifted my leg over the passenger seat, worried the entire load would slide toward me, and hoped for a good outcome to this adventure. Matteo gunned the engine, the motorcycle lost traction in the pebbles and wobbled, I held on tight to both him and the seat, but we found our balance and raced out the driveway and down the hill. Amira held Daisy in her arms and waved goodbye as we took off, her eyes wide, a look of alarm on her face that mirrored my own feelings perfectly.

Every hour we stopped to stretch our legs and straighten our spines. We drove without speaking, bent in half like two tacos packed one inside the other. I felt each of Matteo's vertebrae against my chest every time he shifted his weight, and lost all feeling from my waist down. Every so often, he pointed out something of interest along the side of the road—a baboon troop sunning itself on a cliff ledge, a snake as thick as his forearm slithering across the road to shelter between the boulders, or the tail of an antelope fleeing from the sound of the bike.

On our breaks, we shared water from a screw top jar and ate a little of what Signora Manfriando had packed for us—room temperature egg omelets rolled around fingers of provolone, cherry tomatoes and baby cucumbers from the garden, pine nut cookies.

"There! Lalibela!" Matteo shouted above the engine. Finally. The town first came into view after a four- not three-hour ride. Cranky and sore, I wondered what I was supposed to be looking at. But then Matteo braked and turned off the engine so we could absorb the sight below us. My body continued to vibrate, even after I'd slid off the bike and rubbed my butt cheeks to bring them back to life. There was absolute silence around us except for the motorcycle engine pinging as it cooled. Eagles circled in the sky.

"*Attenta, carina,*" Matteo said. "Look carefully."

He pointed to one side of a village between two mountains and I let the scene sink in. Camouflaged from casual view, primitive churches and steep staircases had been carved right into the sides of the mountains. The late afternoon sun gave a golden cast to everything before us.

Again he indicated, this time to a flat area at the base of the mountains. I realized then what I was looking at—four church complexes carved deep into rock, chiseled out by hand, most of them the depth of a three-story building with the dimensions of a baseball diamond. The doors and windows were below ground level. A narrow alley, the width of a man's shoulders, ran between the churches' perimeters and the scraped-out mountain walls. Carved steps led from ground level down to the church entrances. It was so easy to miss the extraordinary architecture from the road. Alone, I'd have driven right by a World Heritage Site and never noticed it.

Matteo brought me there to witness the Ethiopian Orthodox Church's holiest day of the year, Timkat, the commemoration of the baptism of Jesus Christ by John in the River Jordan. As they had for almost a thousand years, the Christian Orthodox faithful still came to Lalibela from all over Ethiopia to celebrate—thousands of people every year, many of them walking hundreds of miles to get there.

"This is the meaning of devotion…" Matteo said. "*…il significato della devozione.*" He stood there, an unquestioning, if non-practicing, Catholic Christian—silent and moved. His religion was something I rarely thought about. With no Catholic church in Mekele, the Manfriandos spent Sundays worshipping as they always had—at the table. The most they did was say grace.

"A thousand years old?" I asked, awed.

"*Quasi.* More or less. Monks and nuns still live and pray here."

"It's really something."

"It is, *carina.* We will see more tomorrow," Matteo said. "Now we lose the light. *Andiamo!* We need to find a place to sleep."

We got back on the bike and drove slowly down the hill to the town, an even more desolate city than Mekele. It was almost dark on the canyon floor, and the dirt streets were filled with Ethiopian pilgrims wrapped tightly in their lightweight gauze shawls against the night chill.

Matteo stopped again and again, asking in Amharic for directions to a hotel or an inn. We found our way, but there was no space for us at any of them. I didn't mind the thought of spending the night in sleeping bags beside the motorcycle. I actually preferred it. The places Matteo stopped to ask for accommodation were bleak, desperate bars with a few rooms in the back for bar girls and their customers. Even on the evening before Timkat, business seemed brisk.

We stopped at a restaurant with the unfortunate English name of Mussolini's Palace that served both Ethiopian and Italian food. During the Italian occupation, Ethiopians had learned to appreciate Italian cuisine. They especially loved dried pasta. A box of spaghetti with a shelf life of forever—barring cockroaches—an old dented pot, salt, and some boiling water over a small wood fire, kept a caravan traveler's stomach full.

A camel waited out in front of the restaurant, bleating piteously. One front foreleg had been bent up at the knee and bound to its thigh with a thick rope meant to hobble him and keep him from wandering off.

"Camel brake," Matteo said drily.

He threw some coins to a teenage boy with an open, honest face and asked him to guard the motorcycle while we went inside. "This is half the payment," Matteo told him in Amharic. "Same amount later if the bike and everything on it are still here when we return."

At the door of the restaurant, Matteo spoke perfect, educated, Addis Ababa Amharic to the fawning owner. We were seated in the noisy, crowded, and smoky room. Our waiter got over his surprise at finding *ferenji*s in his section and discussed the menu with Matteo. I could have been a ghost, for all the attention the waiter paid to me. They talked a long time, although the menu was limited.

"Two things on the menu tonight," Matteo said to me across the dirty, wooden table. "*Injera* and *wat*…Ethiopian stew with flat bread, or spaghetti with squash, tomatoes, and peppers. Order the spaghetti. It will be spicy, but the *wat* will burn your mouth raw. No water in a place like this; only beer or Coca Cola to drink."

"Spaghetti and a beer," I said, squeamish about all of it. I watched a roach crawl up the wall next to me. "Matteo, look."

"Pray we don't see one in the spaghetti, Anna."

Only men filled the dim, windowless restaurant, eating from a communal dish in the center of each table, stabbing at the air to make their points and shouting at the top of their voices. The serving platters looked like a miniature version of my *tukol*'s straw roof—a colorful striped cone base with a flat basket attached to the pointed top, a foot high off the table. The men used round flat bread, the size and thickness of French crêpes, to scoop up mouthfuls of braised meat and vegetables floating in a fiery, orange sauce that looked dangerous. They ate Arab style, using the right hand only.

I'd noticed that same custom among the factory workers in Mekele. The tailors ate their lunch together, resting on their haunches in a circle in the shade of the flame tree. Lela's kitchen boys ate the same way behind the hotel.

"Why do they eat with only one hand?" I asked.

"They will only touch food with their right hand," Matteo said. "The left is for holding their penises when they urinate and for wiping themselves after they move their bowels."

He looked at my shocked face. "You are surprised?" Matteo grinned. "*Carina*, you're the one who shits off a mountain."

I was. And I lived with roaches and other crawling things nesting in my roof and slithering across my floor.

"And what do you use to wipe yourself?" he asked.

"Smooth rocks and leaves," I said, embarrassed, getting his point. I decided to enjoy the experience without judging. It was my first look at life in Ethiopia without any European influence. We were the only *ferenji*s in the restaurant and possibly in the whole town.

The waiter brought the beer to our table with two cloudy glasses and wiped them with a filthy gray rag.

"Drink from the bottle," Matteo warned me. He grabbed my bottle and wiped it down with his shirt tail. "Ethiopian beer is good." He took both our forks and rubbed them against his other shirt tail with a splash of beer. "Everything tastes better with beer." He looked at me across the table. "You have *coraggio*, Anna. Courage."

I was going to need that courage to eat from the plates of spaghetti and vegetables placed before us. It seemed to be topped with the same orange sauce as the *injera* and *wat*. The waiter smiled nervously, his eyes focused intently on our faces. He stood perfectly still, not breathing, waiting for us to taste our dinners.

"*Spaghetti fa bene, Signore?*" he prodded, his excellent Italian as surprising as Matteo's Amharic.

"*Delizioso!*" Matteo assured him.

"This is horrible," he murmured to me when the waiter turned his back.

I took one bite, and my eyes began to tear, and my nose began to run. I grabbed for my beer like it was an open fire hose.

"I can't eat this," I sputtered. I didn't have words to describe what was

95

happening inside my mouth.

"Don't try," he murmured, ordering two more beers from another passing waiter. "We still have egg and provolone outside on the bike, and more pignoli biscotti."

"I don't understand this," I said. "Why would anyone want their food to hurt them?"

I watched Matteo clean his plate, the large gulps of beer between bites the only indication he was having trouble of his own with the heat. When he was through, he called the waiter over and had a long conversation with him in Amharic that I couldn't understand.

"This is Haile Mariam, a good man," he said, introducing me while shaking the waiter's hand vigorously. Haile Mariam left us for a moment and came back with a tiffin—a tin pail with a screw-off lid, used all over Africa to carry food and water. Matteo scraped my untouched spaghetti into the pail.

"I told him our dinner was so good that we want to save some for later," he said. "We are the only *ferenji*s to eat here in two years, he told me, and I don't want to make him unhappy. He says there are no rooms in town, but he invited us to stay with his family in their *tukol*."

I was a little drunk from drinking my beer so quickly, but I knew I heard right.

"*Coraggio*, Anna," he said again, steering me toward the door with his hand on the small of my back. "It is safer than by the side of the road."

We checked on the bike. Our young guard was asleep, propped up against the front wheel, his shawl over his head, but at least the bike was still there and everything was as we had left it. We waited in a dismal coffee shop next door to the Mussolini Palace for Haile Mariam to finish work. Matteo unpacked the eggs and cookies and brought them inside with us so I would have something to eat with our cups of strong, sugared, syrupy, black coffee. In less than an hour, Haile Mariam walked in, anxious, scanning the dark room for us.

"He left work early to take us home with him," Matteo told me. "He won't make a full day's wages today."

He offered Haile Mariam a coffee, but the waiter was anxious to get home. We figured out how to get the three of us onto the motorcycle—Matteo driving, I came next behind him, straddling the back seat, and Haile Mariam wedged himself sideways behind me. He was respectful, not wanting to hold onto me at the waist from behind, or to force his body against me too closely. He probably weighed less than I did, so the bike balanced nicely as we took off. But it was dark, with no moon, and the road up the mountain was rutted and filled with giant potholes. I held my breath around every turn.

The headlight was the only light anywhere once we left the main street in town, carving shapes and silhouettes out of the darkness. Every ten feet or so, Matteo stopped, steadied the bike with his feet on the ground, and the load wobbled precariously.

After a slow, frightening ride up into the hills that brought sweat to Matteo's forehead and down his spine, Haile Mariam motioned for us to pull off the road.

"My home, it is here, just a short distance from the road," he said. "We must push the bike the rest of the way."

The three of us pushed it between boulders and around rocks strewn everywhere. A rough *tukol*, smaller and more decayed than mine, appeared in the bike's lamplight.

A thin young woman in a long, white, shapeless *shamma* embroidered with a Coptic cross and scrollwork down the front, stood in the doorway, backlit by a weak fire inside, waiting for her husband. She was not expecting two *ferenji*s with him, pushing a motorcycle into their courtyard at that time of night. She probably wanted us in her home about as much as I wanted to be there.

Haile Mariam ushered us toward the door, but Matteo stood firm, for my sake, and insisted we would be fine in the yard. He offered our leftover dinner to the woman, who quickly took it and disappeared inside. Matteo pulled out the tent and our two sleeping bags—Western items Haile Mariam had never seen before and found fascinating. Together they laid the ground cloth, framed the tent, and unrolled the sleeping bags inside.

Haile Mariam ducked beneath the low doorframe of his *tukol* and came back out with a large, heavy stick that he handed to Matteo. "*Protezione,*" he said. Protection. We said *buona notte* and zipped ourselves inside the tent. Haile Mariam made his way to his *tukol* to explain who we were to his wife.

I was tired, but not tired enough to fall asleep. The night was alive with animals. I heard hyenas and owls and all the same sounds of a Mekele night.

"Matteo, I have to pee," I whispered. "Where do I go? I need you to come with me."

"*Coraggio, carina,*" Matteo said, laughing. "This is Africa."

Together we crept out of our sleeping bags, naked except for our T-shirts, and stepped into our boots. We could barely see each other in the profound dark, and Matteo held my hand to keep me close. We tripped over a few rocks, but found a spot behind and away from the *tukol* that Matteo found acceptable, and we peed beside each other. Only three weeks before, I would never have believed myself capable of it. I shivered from the cold and laughed with the thrill of it.

"Come sleep with me," Matteo said, once we were back in the tent. He held the top of his bag open for me and zipped us both in. We lay on our sides; Matteo curled around my back, fingers lightly stroking my breast for comfort, too tired for sex.

"We're like two tacos," I said.

"What's a taco?"

*****

A rooster woke us before dawn, and Haile Mariam's wife, silent, nameless, wrapped in a heavy, white shawl against the cold and dew, brought us two cups of coffee. Not able to see in the dark, I drank the sweet, sludgy coffee without looking at the condition of the tin mugs. When we emerged from the tent, Haile Mariam was sitting against the *tukol* wall, dozing, a grayish blanket over his head and shoulders, his hands around his own cup of steaming coffee, almost invisible in the early morning half-light.

"*Grazie, grazie tanto*," Matteo said to Haile Mariam. He held out his right hand to shake, and in his left he had a few Ethiopian bills. Haile Mariam shook his head under his blanket, refusing the money, but Matteo insisted, pressing the bills into his hand.

"We go now to the rock churches for Timkat. Do you work today? We will come to see you later at the restaurant."

We repacked carefully and headed down the mountain for the holiday. In the light, I was dismayed by the road we'd driven in the dark the night before. Little more than a path, it switchbacked along the edge of a cliff, and some of the potholes were the size of a Volkswagen Beetle.

We could see the churches, and, surrounding them at ground level, was a gathering of hundreds, waiting for the appearance of the priests. We stopped the bike on a dirt path above the churches and a narrow river named the River Jordan, Matteo assured me, and we waited. We sat on the ground cloth, leaning against the motorcycle, eating hard boiled eggs and Italian bread, and watching the sun rise over the churches. Soon the sun was high enough to bake the mountains, the churches, and the mud-brick town.

The Ethiopian priests came through the door of their monastery, adorned in ritual robes of red velvet, thickly embroidered with gold thread. They wore gold filigree antique crowns, hundreds of years old, that sat low on their heads and covered their entire skulls to above their ears. In their hands they carried eight-foot-tall shepherds' staffs of beautifully worked and beaten silver.

They led a long procession of worshippers pushing and jostling each other around the churches and down to the river beneath a canopy of fuchsia, turquoise, purple, and red satin umbrellas with thick gold fringe swinging from the edges. The jewel tones were not the primary colors of Africa, but rather from the bazaars of the Middle East. The trumpet and cymbal music was strange, almost Japanese—nasal and with no discernable beat. Matteo and I scrambled down the hill to walk behind the procession and stood with the faithful on the high banks of the river as the priests blessed the supplicants below.

"These churches, these people…It's amazing," I said, resting my head on Matteo's shoulder. "I wish I knew what it felt like, to have such faith that I could carve a church out of a mountain with my hands."

"Anna? You can have that kind of faith in me."

# 15/ Seduction: Asmara, Ethiopia

At the opposite end of the cultural spectrum was the three-day shopping trip we took to the city of Asmara near the Red Sea. The city could've been any small, coastal city on the Mediterranean, with broad main streets lined with palms, and shade trees that met overhead and cast the sidewalks in deep, welcoming coolness. There were three- and four-story office buildings, boutiques, theaters, bakeries and coffee shops, hotels and restaurants. The salt in the humid air from the Red Sea mixed with the flowering vines and fruit trees that grew in clay pots, and concrete planters created a heady perfume that floated over the city and intensified with every breeze.

The Italians had built up Asmara when they invaded the Eritrean province of the then Abyssinia in the late-nineteenth century, and put the finishing touches on it when they occupied Ethiopia during World War II. Mussolini had offered land and support to entice Italian soldiers and their brides, like the Manfriandos, into settling there. The community that stayed on after the war created a beautiful Italian seaside city that reminded them of home.

Cars whose names and silhouettes I didn't recognize moved up and down the boulevards in an orderly fashion, stopping at street lights and slowing for pedestrians at painted crosswalks. This struck me as novel. I wondered why as I sat in the passenger seat of Matteo's Peugeot, looking out the open window at the city, but then realized I hadn't seen any kind of organized automobile traffic in months. In Mekele, we made our own roads and rules. It was every man, and animal, for himself.

Matteo had reserved a room in the best hotel in the city. The massive building was stone and took up half a city block. An elderly Italian bellman brought our luggage up in an elevator with marble floors, gold leaf, and mirrored walls. An elevator! When he opened the heavy, solid wood, double doors to our room for us with a fist-sized, old-fashioned key on a tasseled cord, I thought I had been dropped into a fairy tale.

The ceilings in the bedroom and bathroom felt two stories tall. They were intricately carved in the corners and gilded with more gold leaf, and the floors were white- and gray-grained marble throughout. The marble bath tub was the size of a hot tub, with *caldo (*hot) and *freddo (*cold) white porcelain water taps, and all the hot water one could possibly want. Living as I did, waiting for the sun to heat the water in my forty-gallon petrol drum to lukewarm, this—and the handheld shower that rested in a caddy at the foot of the bathtub—was the ultimate in luxury.

I studied the bidet, next to the commode, with the extra washcloths and linen hand towels draped over the rim, and asked Matteo why there were two toilets. He laughed and, in his jeans, demonstrated the proper use of a bidet. At that time I didn't even know what it was called. How very civilized.

The huge, four poster bed had a navy-blue and gold jacquard bedspread that was the essence of Old World, over-the-top, Italian décor. The same fabric dropped from the ceiling and formed a half canopy around the four pillows and a full-width, round bolster pillow rested against the headboard. It reminded me of a princess's bed in a castle. I lay back on the bed, sighed, and ran my hands over everything—the Italian jacquard bedspread, the imported soft Italian sheets and, standing in front of me, my handsome Italian boyfriend.

By the side of the bed there was a black, old-fashioned rotary dial telephone for outside calls and room service. Room service! Would there be ice cubes? I called for drinks. A waiter in a black tuxedo jacket brought us two icy bottles of Limonata—an Italian soda made from real lemons—two crystal glasses, and an ornate silver bucket full of ice. I thought to myself, not for the first time or the last, *Italians really know how to live.*

We had brought with us a shopping list two pages long of things to bring back to the Manfriandos, their friends, and Lela from the hotel in Mekele. I had my own list of toiletries I needed and food I wanted to eat—fish and shrimp scampi. We'd arrived in time for a late lunch, so we left the room and headed out to find a restaurant and to shop.

We sat ourselves at an outdoor café down the street from the hotel and Matteo insisted I order branzino, an Italian fish from the Mediterranean and the Red Sea in a lemon, butter, and parsley sauce that was light and elegant, unlike me, as I shoveled it into my mouth as fast as I could. When our plates were clean of every last smear of butter sauce, we watched the pretty Italian girls and impeccably suited men walk by.

For the first time in years, I wanted to wear a summer dress with a full skirt that floated around my knees when I walked, like most of the Italian girls in Asmara. I was wearing my standard Mekele outfit—khaki shorts; an olive military surplus crewneck T-shirt; my tan, scuffed camping boots; and tan, baggy socks. This poor nun wanted a bare dress, her toenails painted, and a pair of high-heeled sandals.

"*Perché, no...*Why not?" Matteo smiled and shrugged his shoulders. "Let me buy you a new dress and sandals and we will find you a beauty salon. Tonight I will take you out to dinner and every man will wonder who you are. *Andiamo, Signorina!* Let's go!"

I had never clothes shopped with a man before. I felt very womanly as we looked through lovely boutiques with imported clothing from Italy and France. Matteo enjoyed the shopping almost more than I did. He patiently watched, with his hands crossed across his chest, as I tried on more than a few dresses, shaking his head yes or no with the smallest of very Italian, impatient head nods and a click of his tongue against the roof of his mouth, sometimes in approval and sometimes in disapproval. Any actual conversation on the pros and cons of each dress was beyond him. But he cavalierly zipped me up and twirled me under his arm, so I could feel the skirts swirl around my legs.

I found the perfect dress—a pale pink cotton sundress with a camisole top and spaghetti straps, attached to a full skirt. It had pink embroidered flowers at the low neckline that continued around the back into a deep V almost to my waist. The embroidery continued in two rows along the back zipper and down the length of the skirt back, all the way to the hem—as pretty from the back as it was from the front. I will never, ever forget that dress. It was the prettiest dress I'd ever seen, much less owned, and I was thrilled as the saleswoman wrapped it in turquoise tissue paper and carefully folded it into a hot pink shopping bag.

I think all girls remember one article of clothing from a time in their lives when they felt their most attractive. That pink dress was it for me. I came out of the glass door swinging my shopping bag, swinging my polished ponytail, swinging my hips like the Italian girls passing us on the sidewalks, and swinging Matteo's hand in mine.

Matteo had asked the salesgirl for a beauty salon where I could get a haircut, manicure, and a pedicure, and she directed us to a shop a few blocks away.

"The beauty salon first, I think," Matteo said. "And then we can shop for shoes. Women's shoes, I love them...but they must be Italian, of course, *naturalmente.*"

Who was this man? My quiet Matteo had turned into a smooth-talking Italian movie star. I hadn't a clue that he liked women's shoes and clothes shopping. At home, he hardly said a word or noticed how I looked. The compliments came from a different place—smoothing the way to sexual favors.

We found the salon and he negotiated for me with the owner—a beautifully dressed, made-up, perfumed, and coiffed older Italian woman with an extraordinary, voluptuous body. She was a mature Sophia Loren type, maybe fifty—old to me then, but I recognized she was also sexy in an ageless way that promised a great deal, simply in the way she moved across a room. She recognized Matteo from when he was a little boy, she exclaimed, and made a huge fuss over him that both embarrassed and pleased him. "I am Signora Marconi. Do you not remember me, Matteo?"

She looked me up and down in my boots and khakis, looked him up and down, and I could tell what she was thinking.

"I have a new dress, Signora Marconi," I stammered, and pulled it out of the shopping bag, wanting her approval.

"*Bellisima*," she agreed, "*Francia*." She knew her fashion provenance without needing to look at the label. "Come with me. *Ti trasformerò in una dea*. I will make you into a goddess."

Matteo left me there in her care while he went to get himself a barber's shave and the first haircut he'd had since I met him.

Two hours later he came back for me, looking like a different man. Just as I had wanted a transformation after an afternoon under the influence of the elegant people around us, he, too, wanted to look better groomed and more...well...Italian. His barber had cut six inches off the length of his hair and combed it straight back off his face. An expert had properly shaved him. He wore a new, white silk dress shirt, untucked; new loafers; and a new pair of soft black trousers that draped just right.

He looked so suave and handsome when he walked through the door that I just sat in my chair, dumbstruck. Signora Marconi made another fuss over him, kissing him over and over again on both cheeks and maintaining full frontal body contact with him through the hips and chest for a good two minutes.

"Ahh, Matteo, *mi amore...Bello come sei...*How handsome you are!"

Had I not been there, I think she might have taken him to the massage room in the back of the salon.

When she let him go, he had a good-sized erection in his new, roomy trousers. I acknowledged it with a raised eyebrow and a smile, and Matteo grinned back at me. She looked him up and down appraisingly one last time, aware of Matteo's reaction to her many, many charms. As we walked out the door, she made him promise to give her regards to his parents.

"*Bello come sei!*" I said, imitating La Signora. "How handsome you are!"

"She's a handful," Matteo admitted.

"I bet Signora Macaroni is the same age as your mother," I said. My response came out of my mouth before I knew what I was saying. Matteo looked horrified for a beat.

"You're jealous," Matteo said, enjoying himself.

"I'm not jealous. I'm...I'm...just...just...jealous." I ran out of steam and admitted it.

"You are beautiful, much more beautiful than the signora," Matteo said. "Let me see your manicure." He took my right hand in his, brought it to his lips, and kissed my palm. "Forget her. Let's go buy some shoes."

Matteo was right to have insisted I get a pedicure, my first pedicure ever, before I tried on sandals. My feet looked beautiful—perfect pink toenails that matched my new dress, and soft heels and soles—and the shoe shopping experience was one drawn-out, exquisite turn-on for us both.

In the shoe store, Matteo sat slumped down in a chair across from mine and watched me try on at least a dozen pairs of shoes until I found the perfect ones—strappy white sandals with pink stones across the instep that matched the pink of my dress and my painted toe nails. He didn't mind at all the time it took to find the right pair of shoes. I knew exactly what was going on with him as he sat there, so low in his chair that he was almost horizontal. He was looking up my shorts every time I stood up, sat down, or put my foot in his lap to show off the shoe, and he was watching my behind and my legs as I wobbled up and down the aisle in high heels.

Matteo squirmed in his chair. I swiveled in my high heels a little closer as I passed him, brushing the tops of his knees with my fingers as I walked back and forth in front of him. He slid down in his chair a little lower, and, at one point, dropped his head in his hands and groaned. He was completely turned on, and I had done it to him.

What incredible power this was, this unabashed feminine power that women like Signora Macaroni understood. I learned the art of seduction that afternoon with every open dress zipper, every toss of my shiny, polished hair, every glossy pink toenail, every backward glance, and every raised eyebrow.

In the late afternoon, after partially making our way through his mother's shopping list, Matteo steered us into a gelato shop. If I hadn't fallen in love with Italy and everything Italian before, I certainly did as soon as I tasted gelato. I hadn't had ice cream in almost a year, but even that couldn't have prepared me for the intense sensation of *gelato limone*. It was, by far, the best thing I'd ever tasted.

I couldn't stand it anymore...not one more minute.

"*Cazza me!*" I whispered into Matteo's ear, between licks of lemon gelato. "No more shopping...let's go back to the hotel...*adesso*...right now."

\*\*\*\*\*

I wore my pink sundress and new sandals that night to dinner in the hotel dining room and I felt just like I'd wanted to feel—pretty, summery, feminine, and sexy. There was soft light from sconces around the walls, an enormous crystal chandelier in the center of the high ceiling, and candles on the tables. I ate my longed-for shrimp scampi, drank my white wine, tasted tiramisu for the first time, and drank a black demitasse from a tiny china cup and saucer, looking around the room, the whole time thinking of Matteo between my legs just an hour before and knowing that, in another hour, he would be right back there again.

We kept track on the notepad by the nightstand of how many times we had sex that weekend—fourteen times over three days. We made up for months of stifled sex with his brother in the bed, or sex in the front seat of the Citroën. I also kept count of the food I ate—six different flavors of gelato and twelve of the biggest shrimp I'd ever seen.

*****

Matteo and I had Signora Manfriando's grocery list and instructions about what to buy from whom—the provolone and Parmigiano Reggiano from this cheese shop, the fresh mozzarella from that one, the sliced prosciutto and pork sausages from this butcher, the veal scaloppini from that one, branzino from this fishmonger, Moscato and Pinot Grigio from only this wine merchant, and the Italian cream pastry from only that bakery. Armed with the list and shop directions, we pulled away from the hotel at ten o'clock in the morning, but didn't leave Asmara until the last shops closed in the afternoon for the *reposo*.

We had brought an ice chest from home, loaded it with ice at our first stop at the butcher, and dropped the perishables in it as we shopped and ate our way across the downtown area. The last stop we made was for one final *gelato limone* before we headed south toward the mountains, Mekele, and home.

We were only an hour outside Asmara, almost to the border between Eritrea and Tigre provinces, when four men jumped out from the dried grass in the culverts on both sides of the road and blocked our path.

"*Mierde*," Matteo cursed under his breath.

All four men were young, excruciatingly thin, shabbily dressed in ripped and filthy army jackets and oversized khaki shorts belted with rope. Their faces were little more than grimacing skulls; jaw and cheekbones jutting from beneath the skin, and furious, menacing expressions. What was more frightening than the machine guns they waved in the air or the manic shouting was the deadness in their eyes.

"*Shiftas*...and they're high on something," Matteo said. "This is not good." He braked very slowly, buying time to think.

"Listen to me carefully, Anna," he said out of the side of his mouth, smiling at the men, taking a long moment before opening his window.

"You're my wife. We live in Mekele. You're pregnant, and we are coming from Asmara after seeing the doctor. If they take me away and out of your sight, I have a loaded pistol under my seat. Go for it and shoot as many of these guys as you can."

"What?"

"Anna, this is serious. Tell me right now that you understand our story and what I want you to do. These men will shoot us as easily as they will let us go."

"I do, I do, but don't let that happen," I said, panicking. "I've never shot a gun."

Two men approached the car on each side, screaming with fury, sweat and spit flying everywhere. Matteo sat where he was and kept both hands on the steering wheel, pretending to be confused by all the men shouting at once. One of the men on my side motioned with his gun that I should roll down my window. I looked at Matteo.

"Do it," he said, "but don't get out of the car."

I didn't understand any of the shouting back and forth in Amharic or Tigrinya. Matteo spoke calmly and didn't provoke them, but he didn't back down either, refusing to get out of the car. He seemed to be playing it just right, displaying neither fear nor aggression. The men calmed down slightly as he spoke. He leaned across the gears to retrieve our traveling papers from the glove box. He handed them to the oldest man, the one who looked like he might be in charge.

"Look," he said. "These are signed by Ras Mengesha." He pointed at the gold Lion of Judah seal on the papers, the seal of the monarchy.

"*Lira, lira, lira!*" the leader yelled at Matteo, demanding Italian currency, waving the barrel of his automatic weapon in the open window. Matteo emptied his pockets of every last bill and coin.

The two men on Matteo's side counted the money and pretended to read the travel documents—front, back, and upside down. One of the men leaned into my window and looked in the back seat. Alcohol fumes and body odor filled the car. The man's eyes were wild and he was soaring on amphetamines. He took note of the ice chest, the cartons and shopping bags stuffed with food, the crates of wine.

The man had raised scars in stripes on his forehead and both cheeks, half a mouthful of yellowed and decayed teeth, and he stank so strongly it made me turn away in disgust. I recovered, looked straight ahead through the windshield, but he turned my chin toward him with the barrel of his machine gun. When he spoke, grinning at me, I gagged from the body odor and the smell that came from his mouth when he shouted at me.

When Matteo saw the *shifta* put his gun in my face, he moved to cover my body with his arms, shouting furiously at the man. The man backed away.

The one in charge decided to let us leave, abruptly indicating with his gun barrel that we should drive off. Matteo turned the key in the ignition and waited while the Citroën rose slowly on its hydraulic chassis. I used to kid Matteo that we could never use his car as the getaway vehicle in a bank robbery, but this was no joke. It felt like it took forever until the Citroën had risen, was in gear, and we were able to drive away.

One of the men, my drunken tormentor, ran after the car, slamming his hand down on the roof for Matteo to stop again. Matteo braked. The *shifta* yanked open the passenger-side door, terrifying me. My heart felt as if it would explode in my chest; surely he was going to pull me out of the car and throw me to the ground and rape me. He pushed past to reach into the back seat, lifting out a few bottles of wine and a shopping bag of groceries.

"Grab the door. Now!" Matteo ordered me. I slammed the door shut as he peeled away, rocks flying.

"What did you say to him to make him take that gun away from me?" I asked, as we drove away.

"I told him if he touched you with even a single dirty finger, I would rip his throat open with my teeth. Then I would bite off his testicles and stuff them in his mouth."

"You'd have done that for me?" I asked, flattered, even in the midst of our escape.

Matteo shrugged his shoulders and shook his head no. "Those are violent men. I just said the most violent things I could think of."

I looked over my shoulder through the rear window at the filthy, doped-up man standing in the middle of the road, holding up a wine bottle in one hand and a white cardboard bakery box tied with red twine in the other— the dinner party guest from hell.

# 16/ Coup: Mekele, Ethiopia

Even in our little town, isolated high up in the mountains, we couldn't escape the political troubles in Addis Ababa. The news of the upheaval in the capital became increasingly dire with each phone call Signore Manfriando received from his old friends in the government. In late August and early September of 1974, we heard of the now-daily strikes and violent demonstrations in the streets. So many professors and students, lawyers and judges, government ministers and civil servants had disappeared or fled the country that there seemed to be no one in control.

What I had witnessed in the taxi when I first arrived in Ethiopia had been only the beginning of the unrest that would topple a three-thousand-year-old monarchy, the longest continuous monarchy in the world. It was all we talked about at the factory and at the Manfriandos' dining room table. We alternated between believing we were safe and untouchable in the mountains, and worrying that the violence would soon come to Mekele's streets.

The emperor handed over the throne to his son, hoping this would appease the protestors and the new army generals pulling the strings. Then he changed his mind and took it back.

Haile Selassie finally agreed to the demands of the Derg, the new Marxist military tribunal, but he was deposed anyway on September 12, 1974. The emperor and the extended royal family were put under house arrest, and the government officials and military officers still loyal to the emperor—the Royalists—were rounded up during the night and jailed, many shot or tortured and never returned to their families.

Around midnight on the night of the coup, Matteo came to my door, banging at it and shouting.

"Wake up, Anna! We need to leave Mekele right away," he said, trying, but failing, to keep the panic from his voice. "Pack only what you really need. Don't light a lamp."

His father had received a phone call at the hotel a few minutes before, warning of the coup and the arrests taking place in the capital and all over the country. Anyone with any influence or ties to the emperor—judges, ministers, lawyers, journalists, provincial governors, doctors, and accountants like Signore Manfriando—was being dragged from their bed and taken into custody. Signore Manfriando was particularly vulnerable; he had been the personal accountant to the emperor and many of the royal family for thirty years and knew where their wealth had been stashed. A billion dollars in Switzerland alone, Matteo confided. A great deal of money that the new regime would search for relentlessly.

This was devastating news for the elderly Manfriandos. As a newly married couple, they had answered a call from their country to settle its new colony with the promise of land and homes and businesses. After thirty years of living peacefully in Ethiopia, they were now forced to flee.

"Hurry, Anna. We have to leave Mekele right *now!*"

"I have to bring Daisy," I said, scrambling to both dress and stuff some things into my duffle bag in the dark.

"Sure, sure...*claro*...just hurry, please. And don't forget your passport."

Matteo understood the threat facing his family. His parents and Tino were hurriedly packing up what they could pile on top of the two family cars while Matteo left to get Gemma and me. Dean was out of the country. His father had died suddenly back in Chicago, so he was safe in America.

Tino would drive his parents and follow Matteo and me south to Addis and hope to get the family on a flight to Europe. There was no other choice. They knew that troops of the new Provisional Army were already arriving in Mekele and that Ras Mengeysha, married to the emperor's granddaughter, had been arrested and taken prisoner. Many of the royal family had been rounded up, and the emperor had been removed from the palace and hidden somewhere.

Matteo told me he had already been to Gemma, but it was too late to help her. The new regime knew about our factory and wanted to keep it viable. Already, there were soldiers around the perimeter of the factory compound and Gemma's home. She was alone and under house arrest. Matteo believed they knew nothing about me. It was really Dean they wanted, as the general manager, but he was out of their reach. In order to ensure his return to Mekele and the continued running of the business, they were holding Gemma hostage.

Ethiopian and Cuban soldiers with machine guns had flooded the capital. Yes...Cuban. The day before the coup, Addis Ababa had been filled with Israeli soldiers/consultants. The next day, Cubans and Russians had replaced them. The new army wore the same olive, drab uniforms with the Red Star patch of the Communists over the yellow Lion of Judah symbol of the monarchy, with different hats, accessories, and Russian-made weapons.

Matteo described the scene at Gemma and Dean's home. Gemma was terrified. When she saw Matteo at her compound gate, she slipped him her passport and made him promise to take it to the British consulate in Addis Ababa. She was willing to give up all proof of who she was in the hope Matteo and I could get her freed. She had entrusted us with a grave responsibility.

I quickly threw together my own passport, my meager safari clothes, my pink sundress from Asmara, some toiletries, and Daisy's leash and water bowl. I left a farewell note and all the schoolbooks for Amira, as well as instructions for the animals. I wrote the note in the dark, crying, knowing Amira would come in the morning, find me gone, and lose hope for her future teaching career. I left her two months' pay and my address in New York.

In another note for the tailors, I explained what had happened and that I hoped their jobs would continue under the new regime. I had my doubts, but to leave them jobless as well as hopeless was something I couldn't do. Matteo sat outside in his Citroën, gunning the engine, anxious to be on his way. We drove back down the hill to his parents' home, and together we loaded suitcases and cartons onto the roof of Matteo's car.

With Tino at the wheel of Signore Manfriando's car, we formed a small caravan and slowly pulled out of their compound as a single unit. The last thing I saw of Mekele, in the circles of light carved by the headlights out of the night, was the family night watchman, covered in his rough, gray blanket, his right arm raised in farewell. I never said goodbye to Lela at the hotel, Dr. Horst and Dr. Sofiya, or any of our other Mekele friends.

"Why are we driving to Addis?" I asked. "Won't that be the most dangerous place we can bring your father?"

"My family discussed this," Matteo said. "The soldiers will be looking for my father in Mekele, if the leaders really have remembered that he has retired here. They may think he has returned to Italy. It's too far a drive to the borders—we'd be on the road for days—and there will be soldiers waiting there, too. My father thought it would be worth the risk getting to Addis and hiding in plain sight with their friends. We'll get my parents on the first Alitalia flight out of the country, hopefully before the traitors even know we're in town."

We drove south through the night on the one paved, north-south road through the country, passing convoy after convoy of Cuban, Russian, and Ethiopian Provisional Army troops. My heart beat so hard I thought it would explode every time we passed those long lines of military trucks, their headlights blinding us on the pitch-black road. I knew at any point the soldiers could have stopped and questioned us. The car lamps of our two-car caravan made us an easy target. If they had discovered who Signore Manfriando was, there is no question they would, at the very least, have taken all of us into custody.

We had escaped from Mekele without drawing attention to ourselves, but we had a long drive ahead of us through the impenetrable dark and a poorly maintained, snaking road, and nothing was for certain.

Matteo had thoughtfully packed a pillow and a blanket for me, and I sat beside him, warm, with Daisy asleep on my lap. I rested my left hand on top of Matteo's as he shifted up and down the gearbox, expertly maneuvering the car around the worst of the gullies and potholes. We were, both of us, hyper-alert all night, our eyes wide, dry, unblinking, and never straying from the small pool of light thrown by our headlights on the road ahead.

We made it safely all the way to Addis and arrived at dawn. We dropped Tino and the Manfriandos off first at the home of Italian family friends. There was a moment, when no one came to open the gray metal double gates, that we thought the family had been taken away during the night. Matteo tapped two times on the car horn, discreetly enough to avoid drawing attention to ourselves, but loud enough to be heard. Finally, a sleepy but terrified *askiri* opened one gate just a fraction, a rifle in his arms. His fear gave way when he recognized Matteo in the first car and the rest of the Manfriandos behind us. He barely opened both gates, looking up and down the street while we drove quickly inside.

The family, the Di Donatos, came to the front door in their robes and slippers, disheveled and half-asleep. After a moment of alarm for themselves, and then recognition, they hurried the exhausted Manfriandos into the house. Matteo and I saw them settled in the kitchen with coffee cups in their hands, and we left the compound again, with instructions where to find the British attaché.

It was only 7:00 a.m., early for the start of a business day, the day after the coup, so we waited in front of the locked and gated office building that housed the British consulate. The streets were empty except for open-bed military trucks tearing around corners, some with sirens blasting through the stillness, some with armed child-soldiers trying to balance themselves while they stood in the truck beds. We sat on the front steps, unsure what we would do if the British attaché failed to appear. We finally saw a middle-aged, overweight, European man heading toward us, approaching the building with quick, short, waddling steps. He was, indeed, the British attaché and he looked very, very worried.

I had been anxious all night that the British ambassador would not believe the story of our journey and Gemma's plight. What would we do if the ambassador refused to take us seriously and Gemma was left stranded in Mekele with no passport or proof of her citizenship? There was no way we could have left her alone in Mekele, but I had no idea what we could do to remove her.

Luckily, the attaché stood before us on the sidewalk, patiently listening and nodding as we told our story, interrupting each other and stumbling over our words. In his fear, Matteo seemed to have forgotten most of his English, his Italian sounding like machine gun bursts. The attaché understood the gravity of the situation before we had even finished explaining it.

"I can't wait to leave this Byzantine country!" he shouted in frustration, his face blotchy with anger and too much exposure to the African sun. His pink skull peeked through his sparse, blond comb-over. I thought it was an indiscreet comment for a diplomat to express in public on the morning after a military coup, but he had probably been up all night, as we had, monitoring the situation for his government, and his nerves were stretched to their limit.

He invited us upstairs for a breakfast of coffee and rolls in his office and allowed us to tell him the whole story of our flight in detail. For the first time since we'd left Mekele, I began to relax as Matteo and I sat together on a couch and ate and drank from a coffee table in front of us. I could feel my neck and shoulder muscles release. Matteo looked exhausted, his eyes bloodshot and rimmed with red, his face drawn, his jaw tense and in need of a shave.

The attaché took Gemma's passport from us and promised he would get her out of Mekele that day.

"I can see how worried you both are, but please, don't worry any more," he said. "I will contact her husband and her family immediately, and see her safely out of the country. This is my responsibility now. I promise you, she'll be fine."

How was he going to make that happen? I looked across at Matteo, but he seemed satisfied.

"Now, you must get to your parents and secure their tickets to Rome as soon as the airport opens again." He handed Matteo his business card. "If you need any assistance, please, contact me. If soldiers come for your father, call me immediately. I will be able to reach the Italian ambassador with one phone call, and the Red Army won't dare touch him. Gemma was clever and quick-witted when she passed you her passport right in front of the soldiers. She is lucky to have friends like you two, willing to take such a risk for her."

Days later, once we were safely out of the country, we called back to the attaché to find out what had happened with Gemma. He told us he had hired a small plane that same morning he found us on his doorstep, flown to Mekele, and ordered the pilot to wait for him and keep the engines running. Using his diplomatic papers and immunity, he removed Gemma right from under the soldier's rifles, escorted her back to Addis, kept her safely and secretly in his own home, and got her onto the first jet out of the country to London.

It was unwise for the Manfriandos to remain in Addis any longer than necessary. Matteo drove us quickly away from the center of the city and back to the Di Donatos'. The city streets were filled with soldiers on almost every corner, but regular people were eerily absent from the streets. It was obvious from the subdued energy in the city that something momentous and fearful had occurred during the night. The entire city was holding its breath.

This time the Di Donatos' Ethiopian *askiri* opened the metal gates to their home as soon as we honked, but he still held his rifle across his chest. My shoulders and stomach clenched tight again.

We had expected to see the Manfriandos' other car where we had left it earlier, right by the front door, but there was nothing in the courtyard. Terrified, and without a word between us, we flew from the car, leaving both doors open, and ran around to the back of the house. The car was there, hidden from casual view with a tarpaulin, the four brown, scuffed leather suitcases still strapped to the roof.

Matteo sank to his knees in relief and buried his face in his hands. They trembled slightly. Yes, he was overwrought from the drive, the tension of the night, and from the meeting with the attaché, and had handled it all with courage and self-control, but this moment in the driveway was his undoing.

"This is so sad," I said, dropping to the ground behind him and putting my arms around his back. I felt his shoulders shudder beneath my palms.

"This is...yes...this is too much..." He stood, back in control, and sighed deeply. "But there's no time to be sad right now." He walked to the car, lifted the tarpaulin, and checked the straps around his parents' luggage to make sure they were secure after the long drive through the country. "We've got to get them out of here as quickly as we can, Anna. I'm very worried for my parents. They're too old. For them, this is too...*troppo difficile.*"

Signora Di Donato came to the kitchen door and waved us in. The Manfriandos were inside, safe, with friends. The two families were sipping at cappuccinos and dipping biscotti at the dining room table as if nothing had changed during the night.

"Come, children, and take a coffee with us." Signora Di Donato welcomed us to the table, unaware of Matteo's meltdown in the backyard. She grabbed his hand and pushed him into a chair. Then I could hear her in the kitchen, pouring the coffee, beating the milk with a rotary beater, and reappearing with two more perfect cups of cappuccino dusted with cinnamon and cocoa powder. She slid the plate piled with chocolate biscotti toward us.

"*Mangia.*"

Of course, when your world is falling apart, eat.

Signore and Signora Manfriando seemed smaller here in Addis, made frailer over the course of one frightening night. Signore Manfriando was confused and unable to make decisions. Matteo sensed he would need to take control right away. He drank his cappuccino—first things first—and left the table to make telephone calls—to the Italian embassy to let them know his family was in Addis and everyone was okay, to the American embassy to let them know I was safe and with his family, to other family friends in Addis to find out their plans and hear the latest rumors, and finally to Alitalia in Italy to book flights home to Rome. The Italian airline was sending extra planes to Addis Ababa to accommodate the displaced expats. Matteo then took his father to the bank, but they came home quickly and very concerned. The banks had not opened that morning.

While they were gone, I called my boss back in the States, Ras Mengesha's partner in the factory, and told him what had happened. He had no idea there had been a coup. I asked him what he wanted me to do.

"Leave...leave now," he yelled through the static of a bad connection. "For heaven's sake, please get out of there and go somewhere safe...and call me when you get there." In my panic and worry for the Manfriandos and Gemma I hadn't really thought things through for myself. The project was over—of course, it was—and I would have to leave Ethiopia.

I then called my parents, hearing them for the first time in almost a year. Listening to their worried voices and feeling a sharp stab of longing for them, made it even clearer to me I needed to go home.

"There'll be more opportunities for you, lots of wonderful adventures ahead," my father said. "I promise you, Annie, this is only the beginning of your life."

My biggest fear was that this was it for me, that I had tried to live my childhood dream of Africa and nothing I would attempt in the future would be as exciting or make me as happy. I felt like I had failed at the business and failed at creating the life I imagined for myself. I could feel through the lines that my dad understood all this, but his words consoled me only a little.

I went to Ethiopia to see what I was made of. I had dreamed of Africa as a child, but didn't know if I had the courage and the strength to live in that world—Jane's world. All my life I had heard my father's words, "If you can dream it, you can make it happen," but I needed to learn it for myself. Who was I? I had never been tested to my limits. Ethiopia was over for me before I was ready.

I understood that my flight from Mekele and the sure collapse of the factory was beyond my control. But I also felt that I was failing the people I had grown to love. I got to go back to my comfortable life in New York while they had to stay where they were, clinging to a mountain cliff, uneducated and starving in the famine. Maybe they were now worse off than when we had arrived. The past year had given Amira and the tailors new skills, the beginning of an education, confidence, and hope for their futures. Would it be enough to carry them forward? Would our hard work

**115**

make any difference in a year?

The African sun would continue to beat down on the earth, the baboons would still steal the people's gasping crops, the rains would come and go, or not, and the wind would blow away all traces of our presence, like dust through the streets. It felt like failure.

# 17/ Flight: Addis Ababa, Ethiopia

Signora Di Donato prepared a lunch of stuffed veal and linguini with chopped fresh tomatoes, basil, black olives, and sautéed garlic. The older couples were frozen with indecision, and the only thing they could think to do was to eat as usual. Signora Di Donato was as good a cook as Signora Manfriando, and no military coup was going to get in the way of a good meal in her home.

The Ethiopian help in the house worked silently around us, eyes enormous with fear, listening to every new rumor the *ferenji*s discussed. When the Di Donatos left Ethiopia, the help stood to inherit all the furniture they had dusted and waxed so carefully for so many years, and maybe they would even be granted the house itself. On the other hand, at any moment they might be dragged outside and executed in the driveway.

All we could do was to wait for the banks to open and the airport to resume international flights. That night, Matteo, Tino, Daisy, and I tried to sleep on the living room couches, but, for the second night in a row, we were unable to let go. Matteo lay stretched out, nerves frayed, dazed, spaced out one minute, and alert the next. A pistol lay in front of him on the coffee table.

Outside the compound walls, we heard more automobile and truck traffic than was usual for the late hour, gunned engines and screeching brakes. Daisy lifted her head once and barked madly, jerking us upright from our dozing. There were no break-in attempts or soldiers banging at the gate, and, in the early hours before dawn, the noise from the streets stopped completely. Even the Communist soldiers of the new Provisional Revolutionary Army needed sleep.

The next morning, business in the city resumed. Matteo again drove his father and Signore Di Donato into the business center of town. They found the banks open, with long lines of frightened customers; Ethiopians and Europeans both. They were able to withdraw their savings in full and then rushed to the Alitalia office to pay for their airline tickets with Italian lira. The Manfriandos had also regularly sent money back to Italy, and I was relieved to know they would not be going home penniless.

They were gone for hours, while the rest of us waited and fretted. Left behind by her husband, Signora Manfriando sat in the dining room all morning, staring out the window at the front courtyard, the flowers, and the palm trees. She said nothing, but accepted coffee after coffee from Signora

Di Donato and never took her eyes from the front gates. I sat with her, but I knew I gave her little comfort.

Tino had stayed with us to protect us and the house from possible looters, and he walked around, peering from all the windows, the pistol from the night before tucked into his jeans' waistband. Every once in a while, he came into the dining room and stood beside his mother, patted her hand, or squeezed her shoulder. She looked up at him each time and smiled weakly, patting his hand in return.

When the honk came, Tino ran outside with Daisy to drag open the gates himself. Only then, when Signora Manfriando saw her husband and son safely behind the compound walls, did she sigh and push herself away from the table. She moved very slowly, as if she was carrying a great weight, shuffling her feet in house slippers, to greet them at the front door.

After another multi-course, two-hour lunch, conversing as though their world had not just collapsed, the Di Donatos and Signora Manfriando went upstairs for their *reposo* and Tino finally fell asleep in the living room.

I helped the young kitchen girl with the dishes and watched from the window above the sink as Matteo and his father sat under a grape arbor, deep in conversation. Their heads were bent toward each other, almost touching, and Signore Manfriando seemed like his old self, his hand on his son's shoulder, talking steadily, obviously guiding and instructing him.

Matteo looked up into his father's face, listening with such deep respect and so much love. I had never seen anything so tender. I understood, then, the depth of the bond between Matteo and his parents. I knew he could never live separately from them. And, I sadly realized in a flash of intuition, that I wasn't the girl for him.

Matteo would be content with a quiet life in Italy, surrounded by his family and centered around his mother's table. That life was not for me. I wanted Africa. I wanted the whole world.

They sat out there, talking for a long time, and then Matteo helped his father out of his garden chair and inside through the kitchen. He found me at the sink, drying the dishes and stacking them in tall piles for the kitchen girl to put away.

"Can we talk about our future, Anna?" he asked with no preamble. He took the dishcloth from my hand and leaned back against the marble-topped counter. "My father and I have been talking and we've decided I can't travel to Roma with them and leave you alone in Addis with no definite plans. Their flight is for tomorrow at noon. We haven't talked about what you want to do. We don't even know yet when you can fly to the States."

He was right. We were so focused on making sure his parents were safe that we hadn't discussed what we wanted for ourselves. When I had called my parents, I knew I had no choice other than to fly home to New

York as soon as I could get a flight. They promised to pay for a TWA ticket and were expecting to hear from me as soon as the airline started flying again. In my heart, I really wanted to stay in Africa and see more, but I had very little money of my own.

"Would you like to come with us now and live in Roma?" he asked.

"Matteo, what are you really asking me?" I said, although I already knew.

"My father and I were talking. He asked me if I want to bring you home with us...if...I want to marry you...*se ti voglio sposare*," he stammered. "It's the right thing to do."

"And what did you tell him?" I was terrified of his answer. I already knew what mine would be.

"Please, *carina*, I don't want to hurt your feelings, but I..."

"It's okay, Matteo, just tell me."

"I don't feel like I have lived enough yet. I'm not ready to marry anyone. But I want to do the right thing for you. If you want to come to Roma now, we can continue the way we are. We can see if we want to get married...maybe...someday." He grabbed a mango from the kitchen counter and nervously tossed it from hand to hand. "My father loves you and thinks we should marry. He thinks it is the right thing to do because we had sex when I knew you had not been with any other man. He is not a modern man, I know that, but maybe he is right."

Poor guy. He looked and sounded like Signore Manfriando was standing behind him, prodding him with a stick, but it was nice, feeling so treasured and valued.

"Matteo, please don't feel guilty about this. I'm twenty-one and I'm not ready to marry anyone either. You need to go home with your family. I want to see the world. Someday, when I come to Rome, I'll find you. Maybe we will want to marry each other then, but maybe you will have settled down with a beautiful wife and a houseful of *bambini*. That would make me happy, too."

He held me to his chest, resting his chin on the top of my head. I could feel how tender he felt toward me, but I could also feel his relief.

"You're a good person, Anna," he said. "I knew I would love you before I even met you...that first day, when I heard you crying in the *tukol*."

"I'm sure you didn't love me then," I countered. "I was just the only girl in Mekele you could possibly sleep with."

"Maybe in the beginning it wasn't love," Matteo acknowledged. "But I knew from the first day that I wanted to protect you from whatever was making you cry."

"You did that," I said. "I stopped crying the moment you put that glass dish of stuffed peppers in my hands and pulled the forks out of your back pocket."

"I have an idea," Matteo said. "I think that, once my parents are out of the country, it will be safe for us to take some time together. I'm sure we'll be safe. It's only a day's drive to the Kenyan border, and I know you would like to see more of Africa before you leave," he added. "We can see my family off at the airport tomorrow morning and then the next day drive to Kenya and down to Nairobi. There's so much to see. I'll ask Signore Di Donato for the Land Rover. We can fly home from Nairobi in a week. We can see the most ancient, colorful Ethiopian and Kenyan tribes and the animals you haven't been able to see in the mountains. You can't go home without seeing a giraffe in the wild."

"Why are you so sure we'll be safe?"

"Why would the militia want either one of us?" Matteo replied. "What they want is for all of us *ferenji*s to be gone. We'll be headed in the right direction."

"You're willing to let your parents fly without you?" I asked. "You would do that for me?"

He nodded slowly, and I could tell he was torn. "Tino will be with them. Once I see them walk through the airplane door, I'll feel better. They have my aunts and uncles and cousins and their friends in Rome—too many of them. They'll be fine without me for a week."

"Perfect." I breathed easier. I never would have asked him to stay behind for me, but I was grateful for this offer and for the time we would have together.

The next morning, Matteo and I drove his family to the airport. Cuban troops and the new Ethiopian military lined the roads leading to the airport; machine guns, ammunition belts, or rifles across their chests. They could pull us over at any time, and we knew it. Signora Manfriando cried softly into her handkerchief, seated between Tino and me in the back seat. I held and patted her free hand, not knowing what else to do to comfort her. The Di Donatos followed us with their guard driving their old Land Rover.

"Thank you, Signora, for all your kindness and for everything you've taught me," I told her in my best Italian. "I'm so grateful and I'll never forget you."

What I think she answered me back was, "No, no, no. I thank you for making my son so happy this year. You've learned to cook very well. You are like a daughter to me...*come una figlia per me.*"

She had steadily been shrinking over the last two days, and, as she held onto Matteo at the gate, she seemed no bigger than a garden gnome. They both cried openly.

Tino kissed me goodbye on both cheeks and whispered, "All the times you and Matteo thought I was sleeping? I was awake for all of it."

I laughed. Matteo looked across at me strangely.

"Come and visit us soon in Italy," Signore Manfriando said to me, very formally, but then he took me in his arms into a big hug.

He embraced his oldest son and offered some last-minute instructions quietly in his ear. He let out one final, deep sigh of disappointment and turned to walk stiffly across the tarmac to the plane. The last two days had aged him and he now carried himself like a very old man. A lifetime in Ethiopia—a choice for adventure made in his youth with a young and willing wife, the excitement of his work as a trusted advisor to an emperor—all of it now gone.

The other passengers pushed past the soldiers at the gate and ran to the plane. Only the older, slower folks were left to manage as best they could. Signore and Signora Manfriando, leaning on Tino, were the last ones up the stairs and through the door, dragging our hearts along with them. Tino turned to wave at us when he reached the top. "It'll be okay," he seemed to say to Matteo. "I've got this."

Matteo was silent and tense as we drove back to the Di Donato compound, looking neither to the left nor the right at the soldiers in the street, not daring to breathe deeply until the metal gates were shut and locked behind us. We had promised to organize a big house cleaning, pay the staff a month's wages each, and take some packed boxes to Ethiopian friends who lived nearby—an afternoon's work.

Signora Di Donato had taken their family photo albums with her, but their lovely tableware and silver, and their collections of books and records had been left behind. She wanted them to go to a colleague of Signore Di Donato's, an Ethiopian engineer, whose family compound was only a few streets away. The clothing and shoes remaining in their closets were to be divided up between the household help.

We noticed as soon as we pulled up to the house that cartons had been packed and stacked in the front hallway, waiting for the Land Rover. The household staff appeared from their quarters behind the house and stood quietly, watching us, waiting for news—the day guard and the night watchman, the gardener, the handyman, the cook, the kitchen girl, and the housemaid. They had questions and they deserved answers. Signore Di Donato had prepared envelopes with cash for each of them with goodbye notes from the Signora. Matteo handed them out in the kitchen.

"The Signore and the Signora want you to have this money for your families. You are free to return to your villages in the countryside or to remain here in your quarters. The new government will certainly take the house and the furniture for one of the new ministers or generals. It is probably best for your own safety that you don't disturb much, but the Signora wants each one of you to choose something from the house for yourself."

"This house is my only village. I have nowhere else to go. I will stay here until I am forced to leave," said the day guard. "I will protect the house."

"You are welcome to stay, but don't put yourself in danger protecting the house when the soldiers come," Matteo warned. "Signore Di Donato doesn't want you to do anything that will bring you to the attention of the soldiers."

"When do you and the signorina leave Addis, Signore Matteo?" asked the cook. "Do you think we can share between us the remaining food in the pantry and the freezer?"

"We are leaving in the morning for Kenya. We have permission to take the Land Rover, but I will give you my Citroën and teach you to drive it after dinner. Yes, share the food among you before it spoils. All we need is dinner tonight, breakfast in the morning, a basket for the journey, and the rest is yours."

"I will prepare a box of food, water, and supplies for you, for your safari," he offered. "Kenya is too far and many days' driving."

"That is very kind of you," Matteo said gently, tears welling in his eyes.

The cook had prepared a simple lunch for us, following the normal household routine—spaghetti tossed with vegetables from the garden, a salad, and garlic rolls like Signora Manfriando used to make. We had sliced mango and papaya for dessert. Matteo ate with a better appetite and talked fondly about his childhood in Ethiopia.

"We had horses we kept in a field behind our house," he told me. "One of them, Gogo, was so smart he could always figure out how to get out of his stall. If we left the window to the stall open, he'd put his head through and unlock the latch. If we added a second lock, he figured out how to open that one, too. We used to find him in the morning, grazing on the lawn or in the gardens. My mother would chase him, flapping a dishtowel in his face. No matter what we tried, Gogo found a way to escape.

"He was a great, *gigante* horse, but gentle with Tino and me. When we were very little, our gardener would lead us around the yard on Gogo's back whenever we begged. My mother has a picture of me somewhere, sitting on Gogo, a long, long way from the ground, naked except for my diaper, my legs sticking straight out from his flanks."

"It sounds like you had a lovely childhood here," I said.

"*Sì*, Anna. An African childhood is the very best kind…so much for a boy to get into, and so much love from everyone in the house. I would never have wanted to grow up any other way." He took a last sip of his espresso. "Now, come lie down with me for an hour, and then we'll take care of the errands."

We collapsed on the freshly made bed in the guestroom and slept for the first time in two days. It was 6:00 p.m. before we jolted awake at the same moment, wondering at the unfamiliar room in dusky shadows, before the memory of the last two days crystallized in our minds.

# 18/ Beautiful: Southern Ethiopia and Northern Kenya

Matteo and I left the Di Donato's Addis Ababa home early in the morning, before dawn. We had packed their old Land Rover tight with camping equipment and a supply of water, petrol, bread, biscuits, fresh fruit, and vegetables. Their cook had come in early to prepare a huge breakfast that would keep us full for most of our first day on the road. The entire staff stood on the front steps and waved to us forlornly as we passed through the compound gates. The house and its interior belonged to them now.

It was a sad ending, a sad goodbye to Ethiopia and the past year in the Mekele mountains, but it was a guilty relief to leave Addis Ababa and the aftermath of the coup; the sudden bursts of gunfire, the long lines of fleeing people along the roadside, the blood still wet in the streets. We had the road ahead of us through the southern lands of primitive Ethiopia and over the border to Kenya's mostly undeveloped Northern Territory land. We were on a safari through the landscapes of my old Africa scrapbook.

We drove through the outlying suburbs of Addis, and, as the road became narrower and more and more pitted, it gave way to a few small towns and even smaller Ethiopian villages. Inside of half an hour, we left behind a modern city and discovered a world from a thousand years ago.

We began to see more wildlife—more in a day then I had seen the entire previous year. Zebras, antelopes, wildebeest, and even giraffes began to appear. Hippos and crocodiles hugged the lake shores. A six-foot long black mamba snake hung in loops from a tree branch right beside the road. I'd seen large snakes in Mekele, but never one as tall as a man and as wide as his forearm.

"Look, Matteo! A baby elephant...oh, look! A pride of lions on that rock. Stop, stop! The giraffes are waiting to cross the road." I rode with my head out the window or through the sun roof and pointed out everything I saw through the binoculars. Matteo pulled the Land Rover to the side of the road over and over again so I could really see the animals, even though we hadn't yet reached the safety of the Kenyan border.

"Now, Anna, this is Africa, no?" Matteo asked. He was so glad and proud to be able to give this to me.

"Yes, oh, yes!" I said. "It's what I've been missing all this time."

A whole new Africa opened up to me.

"We'll see tonight when we make camp in the bush if you still feel that way."

"The animals must be more scared of us than we are of them," I said, repeating what I'd been told my whole life about animals.

Matteo shrugged. "Who says that? No one in Africa would say that."

The villages we passed through were composed of a main street, barely paved or not at all, with the small shops like the ones we left behind in Mekele. Sandal makers, tailors, and barbers conducted business on the wood-planked, dusty sidewalks, and the general stores, tea shops, bars, and butcher shops did business from shops made from mud bricks, painted bright colors—two-tone turquoise and white, green and white, yellow and black, red and yellow—the colors of Africa.

Beaded jewelry and brightly printed fabric lengths for clothing wraps were hung on rods or pinned to clotheslines and displayed in the open air, catching the rare breeze and brilliant in the sun. Intricately woven straw baskets, specific to the tribe in each village we passed, were piled high on plastic tarpaulins spread out on the dirt. Vegetables, fruits, and spices in large, open canvas bags also lay on tarpaulins or old newspaper. The country women squatted patiently behind their produce and did a day's business a penny at a time.

The people we passed became stranger and wilder. As we drove further and further south, pieces of their clothing became less and less Western. Second-hand Western T-shirts gave way to bare upper torsos—women as well as men. Threadbare khaki shorts disappeared almost entirely, replaced with coarse cloth or tanned animal hides wrapped around the hip. Many of the women we met wore beaded leather belts with front flaps for modesty, nothing in the back and nothing on top.

The hair ornamentation became more and more extreme—bones and tusks, seed pods, string, beads, safety pins; they used almost anything they could find to decorate their hair. Gone were the swirling, neatly braided hair styles of northern Ethiopia, the white clothing, the strings of chunky amber beads, and silver Coptic crosses.

Matteo pointed out people from the different tribes we passed along the road. The Karo tribe painted their faces and limbs white with a mixture of ash and lime. They lined their torsos with horizontal brush strokes and dots, wonderful geometric patterns that were striking against their dark, dark skin. Their arms and legs were sometimes covered with the same short, horizontal lines. Primary-colored plastic beads strung on narrow copper wire were formed into necklaces and bracelets and were worn by both men and women, stacked up their arms to their elbows, and up their necks from shoulder to jaw. They wore little else besides a small tanned animal hide or a length of coarse fabric wrapped around their hips.

The Abore tribesmen also painted their dark faces with white, quarter-sized polka dots in swirl patterns and concentric circles, accentuating the eyes and mouth. Some added yellow or red dots to the patterns; so simple and yet stunning. It was as if the Abore had a natural sense of style and beauty.

The Hamers loved red; dried red mud coated their faces, their limbs, even their hair, braided around cord and then covered with more mud. Some cut bangs and turned their headful of braids into a kind of pageboy hairstyle made completely from the narrow braids. They loaded themselves up with beaded bracelets and necklaces, tin and copper cuffs, and wrapped themselves in red cotton or beaded leather slim skirts.

The Mursi tribe was the most disconcerting and took some time getting used to. They inserted round plates into pockets cut beneath the lower lip so they protruded out from the face. The plates were flat—wooden disks, beaten copper or tin, or decorative and painted in red and other primary colors —and sometimes they were the size of the entire face.

Both men's and women's earlobes were opened into long drooping holes that held more decorative plates. From early childhood, small twigs were inserted into small pierced holes in the earlobe, with wide and then wider branch sections inserted over time to create holes that, eventually, could accommodate the larger and larger disks. Sometimes they fell below the shoulders.

The Mursi practiced scarification on their faces and bodies. Ash residue from cooking fires was rubbed into open knife cuts on the skin, leaving raised welts that healed as darker geometric or swirling designs. One young woman we saw had raised dots encircling her beautiful breasts in concentric circles, meeting at her sternum and separating again to encircle her hips. The Mursi decorated their hair with all manner of small items: shells, pompoms, child's tin clip barrettes in bright colors, bits of metal scraps. The weight of so much ornamentation in their hair must have made holding the head up a difficult task. Then, for a final flourish, they often hung warthog tusks or antelope horns on either side of their faces, making them look dangerous, frightening, and unknowable.

Once on the Kenyan plains of the Northern Frontier, we began to see the Masai and Samburu. The two tribes were closely related, and both were nomadic in their lifestyle, moving across the land with their cattle and goats. They were often in the villages with their herds of livestock. The men were the peacocks and the women were drab by comparison. The women's heads were shaved smooth and rubbed with red mud, and they wore simple leather skirts and only beaded necklaces and earrings. The men, however, were a whole other thing. They wore their hair long, braided around string and reaching past their shoulders like dreadlocks, sometimes with a braided fringe across their forehead. The dried mud made the braids stand out stiff from the head, very much like an Egyptian head-dress. In the sunlight they looked like they had bright, orange-red hair.

The Masai and Samburu both favored a simple red and white checked fabric knotted at one shoulder, and adorned themselves with armfuls of beaded bracelets, necklaces, and headbands. Some even wore makeup like the men from ancient Egypt; black kohl lining the eyes. They seemed very effeminate, but they carried spears and long shields, and looked willing to use them.

These tribesmen were truly frightening to me at first, but then, as we passed more and more of them in the towns and villages as we stopped for petrol, Cokes, beers, and fruit, I slowly came to see their beauty for what it was.

They were all beautiful in their own way. They used their bodies and faces as canvases for stunning artwork and their hair and earlobes as foundations for sculptures. They carried themselves with elegance and grace, straight and true and slim, heads balanced high on their long, taut necks. Most had brilliantly white teeth that stood out against the contrast of their dark skin. The elderly may have lost their teeth, and their skin may have been wrinkled, their bodies stooped, but they still walked miles and miles each day and seemed healthy.

Their emotions were easy to read through their painted faces—joy, fear, happiness, curiosity, confusion; just like ours.

As we leaned against the truck while we pumped petrol one afternoon, three young Hamer teenage girls walked past us with their arms around one another's waists. They were coated in dried red mud, from their plaited pageboy hairdos down to their ankles and feet. Their forearms and ankles were cuffed in brass, beaded at the edges, and trimmed with cowhide strips. They wore short leather skirts around their hips, and nothing above but masses of colored beaded necklaces that hung from their necks and beaded leather headbands adorning their foreheads. Their naked breasts were beautiful; high and firm. They were decked out, Hamer-style, like Western teenagers ready for a Saturday afternoon at the mall.

They stopped chattering when they passed us, stared, and continued down the dirt road, giggling and looking over their shoulders. Moments later they returned and approached us. The bravest of the three came up to me and said something undecipherable. She touched my hair, which was tied back in a long ponytail that hung down below my shoulders, and stroked my mosquito-bitten white skin in wonder. She swung my ponytail back and forth like a bell and the other girls laughed. Matteo went inside the gas station office and came out with cold Cokes for all of us. It wasn't clear whether they had ever had Coke before, but it was very clear how much they loved it.

What must they have thought of me, a young woman almost their own age? How drab I was in comparison; no color to my pale skin except a sunburned flush, no color or decorations in my hair except a red rubber band holding my ponytail together, no face paint, no jewelry, my body almost completely covered in a khaki T-shirt, baggy pants, and heavy camping boots on my feet. They were like brilliant parrots, and I was a drab pea hen. I may have been cleaner, but how beautiful they were and how creative.

I dressed almost every morning in the same style clothes and combed my hair into the same ponytail—sometimes a high one and sometimes low. The Hamer girls woke and decorated themselves differently every day, made their own jewelry, tanned and decorated their leather skirts, created new hairstyles.

I had bought strings of cowrie shells and clear bags of small, primary-colored plastic beads earlier in the day from a stand along the road. I took them from the glove compartment and gave them to the girls before they left.

"Do you find them beautiful?" I asked Matteo, after the girls walked away, arms around each other as before.

"*Bellissima*," Matteo said, looking after them. "Their bodies are beautiful, but I don't desire them, if that's what you're asking. They are beautiful, but like a sunrise…only to watch."

"I feel like a rock or a twig next to them…like nothing," I admitted. "They're so extraordinary."

"Italian men like rocks and twigs," he said. "But maybe with a little lipstick."

\*\*\*\*\*

We traveled for three nights and four days, taking our time on the road once we crossed the border and were out of the reach of the Ethiopian Revolutionary Army. The first night, we camped by ourselves in the bush, pitching our tent in the middle of nowhere. We made a fire and roasted large potatoes and whole onions from the Di Donatos' pantry and then mashed them together. I was afraid to be so exposed, but the animals never bothered us. Matteo kept an enormous fire going all night. We fell asleep together in my sleeping bag, listening to the sound of monkeys swinging from the tree branches above our heads as they settled for the night in the leaf cover, and we woke at dawn to birdsong.

The second day, we crossed the border at Moyale and on to the town of Isiolo in Kenya. There we hired a guide to take us through the Samburu Reserve for a day of amazing animal watching—giraffe, lion, elephant, wildebeest, gazelle, ibex, and impala. We saw a magnificent cheetah that day, just standing in the middle of the dirt road staring at our Land Rover. It never moved for us; this was the cheetah's home and we were the intruders.

We stayed the night at the Samburu Lodge in a king-sized bed beneath white mosquito netting while monkeys scampered across our deck and along the deck's wooden railing. The sliding glass doors to the viewing deck had to stay shut or we would have had a room full of monkeys.

The third afternoon, Matteo found us a tented camp to stay in that operated for the safari tourist trade. Stationary canvas tents had been raised on square cement platforms with the relative comfort of toilets, showers, sinks, and hot water, giving the tourists the experience of true safari camping without the hassle of digging a latrine, building a campfire, or cooking their own food.

The manager let us pitch our tent on an empty platform on the outskirts of the property and invited us to take our meals with him and his guests. We spent a lazy afternoon drinking tea and eating ice cream from deep soup bowls. Ice cream is hardly a staple safari food, but, at the camp, the kitchen was as stationary as the private tents. There was even a good-sized vegetable garden. We relaxed in canvas camp chairs at the long, outdoor dining table set up beneath huge baobab trees and watched wildlife through our field glasses. Zebra grazed the grass among the rock outcroppings, and giraffe reached for leaves in the sparse trees only a hundred feet away from where we sat. We had the camp to ourselves while the paying guests were out on a late afternoon safari drive.

The manager joined us at the table for a quick break before his guests arrived back and dinner service began.

"Two female rhinos with a baby came through here two mornings ago and did some damage," he told us. He was a tall man in his forties from New Zealand, with a strong New Zealand accent. "Tore down a few tents and sent some folks running from their tents with no shorts on." He laughed at the memory, now that the very serious danger had ended safely. "There's a river a short way from your side of the camp, maybe half a kilometer. The rhinos went off in that direction, so keep an eye out for them tonight. They're probably not that far away."

There were no barriers between the animals and the camp, no rule about staying inside one's vehicle as there was for the government-owned national parks. The wildlife was free to graze as they wanted on this private land owned by the Masai tribe.

"Any lion around?" Matteo asked.

"Indeed! One group of tourists saw a whole pride this morning, right after a fresh kill. The guests were excited about it at lunch. They got their money's worth today," the manager said. "Do you care to go out for a look? I can send a guide out with you."

Matteo looked at me for agreement before he answered. "We've been driving for two days. We've seen lots. We'll just sit here for a while. Can we use the pool before your guests return?" Yes, there was a pool at this safari camp; a bit basic and scruffy, but an unheard-of luxury in the bush.

We had no swimsuits with us, but Matteo wore his shorts, and I wore my underwear and a T-shirt. We cannonballed into the water, brushed aside the leaves floating on the surface, and let loose. It was the first and only time Matteo and I swam together. We would be parting soon, and it felt good to forget about it and just play in the water like children. A dozen unperturbed zebra grazed beside us, and a spindly baby pranced about, kicking his feet in the air, like us in the pool, with the joy of being in Africa, the joy of being alive.

The last evening, we could have pressed on and made it to Nairobi before sunset, but we decided to spend one more night on the road at a lodge along the shore of Lake Naivasha. When we arrived, thousands of flamingos in the lake had turned the horizon bright pink in the fading daylight against a sunset sky of orange and crimson.

We drank wine with the other guests in the bar and ate dinner, just the two of us, by candlelight, looking across the lake. I dressed up for Matteo one last time in the pink sundress and the sandals we had bought in Asmara.

In the morning we would drive the short distance to Nairobi, we would find Matteo's Danish friends, and he would make plans to fly to Rome, but for this final night of our trip out of Ethiopia, in that romantic lodge, we could take all the time we needed to say goodbye to each other properly.

# 19/ Farewell: Nairobi, Kenya

By the time we reached Nairobi the next afternoon, I knew Matteo was more than ready to say goodbye to Africa. He was tired of four days of driving, tired of sweating through his shirts and shorts, of being covered forehead to boot tops in road dust and sweat, of being sunburned and parched. He was tired of the African sun itself. For me it was different. I hoped for a miracle that would allow me to stay.

Nairobi!

We drove through unknown, and yet thoroughly familiar, streets. I was amazed I was here. The girl who sat on her bed and flipped through her scrapbook for the thousandth time? The one who read Isak Dinesen's *Out Of Africa* when she was eleven years old? That was me. I marveled, watching the city from the open Land Rover. Could a person really have their dreams come true once and then come true again and again? Addis Ababa had prepared me for this great African city, and it was everything I had imagined as a child—the colors, the sounds, the smells, the light.

Nairobi sat eight thousand feet above the Indian Ocean, on the earth's equator and closest to the brilliant sun, which made everything crystal clear and gilded golden. I felt I could see clearer and further than I ever had.

Nairobi!

The comforting smell of charcoal cooking fires; the perfume of mangos and bananas left out in the sun all day; of tropical flowers from vines and trees and shrubs; the dry, dusty odor of dirt; the gasoline fumes from diesel mini-buses and prowling Mercedes; the stench of animal carcasses and desiccated feces.

Nairobi!

The sounds of the city were a disharmonic symphony of bleating donkeys, goats, and camels; cow bells; the heavy beat of African music spilling from bars; the honking horns and squealing brakes of buses and taxis against a modern city backdrop of glass-walled office towers, banks, restaurants, and galleries.

Nairobi!

There were people on the city streets in every possible combination of Western and tribal dress—tanned animal hides, African prints from all over the continent, dashikis, turbans, Indian saris and tunics, red and white checked fabric, and filthy red blankets. The African women wore brightly colored, plastic beaded necklaces, earrings, and bracelets, and the men carried handmade spears and shields—the complete opposite of the stately, austere Ethiopians in their white cotton shawls and hammered silver jewelry. Many wore their hair in tightly braided corn rows, like Ethiopians, but many more covered their long, braided hair or shaved scalps with red clay.

There were embassy and Non-Governmental Organization workers and government officials from all over the world in business suits and polished wingtips; safari tour guides and expats from the surrounding fertile farmland in khaki vests, short-sleeved shirts and long shorts. Muslim women floated by like charcoal ghosts, covered from head to toe in black burqas, and women from the countryside walked barefoot and topless, wearing narrow, leather-beaded skirts to their ankles, baskets of produce on their heads or firewood strapped to their backs.

Nairobi!

Matteo had got us from the mountains of Ethiopia, across a thousand miles of wildness, to the highlands of Kenya, without once looking at a road map, but we were lost in this city with its mad contrast between the bush and the modern, high-rise office buildings and banks. He turned left and then right, hoping a street name would sound familiar, then gave up when we passed the gates to the famous Norfolk Hotel. He left the keys with a valet, and we walked into the hushed and air-conditioned lobby to find a phone to call his friends for directions—a very city-like thing to be able to do.

Our safari ended when we pulled into a dirt driveway on the outskirts of town and parked in front of a small, thatched-roof bungalow surrounded with overgrown palms and chaotic, towering, flowering vines and bushes. When Matteo shut off the engine and the smell of diesel fuel evaporated, I was overwhelmed by the gorgeous smell of jasmine and gardenias growing against the front wall.

Matteo's friend, Benni, large, like a giant, smiling blonde bear, came out the front door to greet us, shirtless and in baggy shorts. He was a well-known photographer in Europe, successful enough to move his family anywhere in the world they wanted to live. They had lived in Addis Ababa for five years and had moved to Nairobi less than a year before. Farah, Benni's friendly, curly-haired, blond wife, followed with their young son, David. They were Danish, dazzling with the good looks and great energy that come only from healthy living. Before Matteo could slide out of his seat, Benni grabbed him and lifted him out of the driver's seat and up into the air in a huge, light-hearted embrace.

They welcomed us into their home the African way—graciously, as if we'd known each other all our lives—and showed us first to their simple, spare bedroom, offering it to us for as long as we wanted to stay. Farah handed me a mountain of pillows and linens that smelled of lavender, a charcoal-heated iron, and old-fashioned laundry starch. Her houseboy took our duffle bags from us, dumping the contents into a 1950s washing machine on the back porch. He came again for Daisy and took her to the backyard to introduce her to the two family dogs. Matteo and I made up the narrow bed together, happy to have been integrated so easily into such a warm and inviting home.

Benni and Farah's single indoor bathroom had a small shower, inconsistent hot water, and a porcelain toilet with a water tank on the wall and a pull chain for flushing. We showered and came to dinner with the African bush and road dust washed out of our hair, clean clothes, and with enormous appetites. We devoured bowl after bowl of vegetable soup, two loaves of sunflower and pumpkin seed bread with the freshest butter, and a pyramid of tiny strawberries that were the size of my thumbnail for dessert.

They wanted to know the latest news about the coup in Addis, our escape, the whereabouts of mutual friends, the new military council in charge, and the arrests still happening throughout Ethiopia. They had been reading all about it in the Nairobi newspapers and were keen for our firsthand information. We sat comfortably around the table in the old-fashioned kitchen until late into the night, with the moths and mosquitoes hurling themselves at the mesh screens in the windows and immolating themselves in the candle flames.

Now that our journey was over, Matteo became anxious again about his family. Over coffee, he admitted his desire to leave for Rome right away—the next day, if possible. I said nothing about my own plans. I looked at Matteo, realizing with a shock he might be gone by the following night.

"You're not going to Rome with Matteo?" Farah asked me as we washed the dinner dishes.

"No," I admitted. "I don't think there's enough between us. I'm just not sure…"

"Poor Matteo," she said. "His girlfriends always leave him. He chooses sweet girls and he knows how to love them, but he doesn't know how to make them love him back."

"I didn't know…" I stammered. I knew nothing about Matteo's past relationships and, reluctant as he was to talk about himself, he had never brought them up.

He was my first love, and, because I had chosen a good man, I knew nothing yet of losses and regrets, of humiliation or self-doubt. What I did comprehend, standing there in Farah's kitchen, was that he had been hurt before, and I was hurting him again. My heart broke for him, for the shock of our final hours, and I began to cry.

Farah sighed, understanding everything.

"How am I supposed to know if he's my future?" I asked, weeping into the dishtowel.

"It's very simple, Annie. Do you feel you are a better person because of him?"

"I know he's honorable and sincere, and he's so brave. And I'm more courageous, more confident, and more appreciative of my surroundings because of him," I said. "But sometimes I felt smothered in his home, and that doesn't make me feel like a better person at all. His family is so loving, so accepting of me, but I've been jealous of the time he spends with them and away from me, and I don't like that about myself."

"Matteo's a good man," Farah said. "He'll make a good husband."

"I know, but he has no skills, no career goals. His only passion is the family vegetable garden. And sex. And his mother's cooking."

"Come on, Annie," she admonished me. "He's very good with cars and motors. He kept our old Land Rover running the whole time we were in Addis. And he always refused to take any money for all the work, not even for the parts. He's been a good friend to us and we love him."

"I love him, too, but I'm twenty-one and I don't want to be a girlfriend or a wife stuck in my in-laws' home," I sobbed. "I don't want to scurry down a mouse hole before I've explored the world. There's so much I want to do, so many places I want to see. All this! Africa. And Europe. Asia. Indonesia. Antarctica, even."

"Benni and I have been all over the world," Farah said. "But there's no place more important to me than this little bungalow and my family. Wherever they are, that is where I am the happiest. And, by the way, Rome is hardly a mouse hole."

"You're right," I agreed. "But even Rome will start to feel like a mouse trap if I'm not happy. Matteo wants his life to stay as it is. His family gives him a sense of security. He's slept in a bed with his brother since they were babies and he brought me to that bed. I learned how to make love to him with Tino in the bed beside us."

"No!"

"Yes!"

"But that won't happen in Rome," she assured me. "What happens when Tino brings a girlfriend home? Will Matteo expect the four of you to share the same bed?"

Of course not, but the thought only made me cry harder and feel worse about myself. I knew I wasn't willing to take the chance that Matteo would find his way to manhood, to a career, to the head of his own family. He hadn't proposed, I had to remember, and had been prodded by his father to offer to bring me back to Rome with the family. I couldn't believe he would have come up with the idea on his own.

"What are your plans, then?" she asked. She was kind enough to change the subject when she saw me so sorrowful, so crushed.

"I want to stay in Africa, but I don't know how," I said, sniffling, but calming down. "I'd like to see more of Kenya, but the only money I have is what I saved in Mekele—not much. Maybe I have enough to stay for two or three weeks."

"Well, you can leave Daisy here with our dogs and you can come and go from our house," Farah smiled. "We can all take some time off and take you into the bush. We haven't been on a family safari in quite a while. Benni's just got home from shooting a project on chimpanzees in Uganda, but I know he'll want to go. He and David are always happiest away from the city."

"That will be wonderful." My spirits lifted, grateful for the offer and a glimpse into a future beyond Ethiopia. "I haven't seen the Indian Ocean yet, so I'd also really love to go somewhere on the coast."

"I know the most perfect place—Lamu, an island off the coast of Mombasa—and the most wonderful beachfront hotel that's not expensive. Oh, Annie...it's heavenly."

"Maybe Matteo will want to come, too."

Farah fixed me with a stare and raised an eyebrow.

I understood that I couldn't have it both ways. I could have Africa or I could have Matteo. I chose Africa and I knew then that, somehow, I would return.

We wiped off the counters, folded the dishtowels over the lip of the sink, and turned out the bare electric light in the kitchen ceiling.

"Go to him, Annie," Farah encouraged. "He's so sad. I can tell."

Matteo was in Benni's studio, sitting in a worn-out armchair, reading from a small printed schedule of flights out of Jomo Kenyatta airport.

He looked up at me. "There's an Alitalia flight out to Cairo with a connection to Rome tomorrow afternoon at one o'clock that I want to make."

"Well, then, come to bed with me, Matteo. Every moment we have left counts."

"*Sì, carina. Andiamo*...let's go. This is true. Every moment counts."

"I'm so sorry," I said, crawling in beside him beneath the covers on the single bed. I fit my head in the space between his neck and his shoulder, and the rest of my body along the length of his. This, I would miss—how the curves and planes of our bodies lined up and slipped into place against each other. He was a foot taller than I was, but lying down we fit together seamlessly.

"I understand, Anna," he sighed. "I really do. What I have to offer you is not enough..."

"No, don't say that!"

"Okay, Anna…Okay. No more talking."

We moved together without any more words. We'd already said goodbye and everything else we needed to say to each other in the safari lodge on the shores of Lake Nakuru. We slept badly in the narrow bed, disturbed by the dogs and by our kicking legs and thrashing arms, waking again and again, not recognizing where we were and then remembering everything. During the night, we had sex every time we woke, sharing a final need to feel connected.

In the morning, we packed Matteo up with whatever we thought he could use in Rome. Everything else—the tent, the lanterns, the oil lamps, the tin teakettle and soup pot, the canteens, the binoculars, even the rifle and the pistol—he left for me.

"You'll need all this," Matteo said. "You'll be back."

*I will*, I thought.

"You have my parents' address…and their phone number?" I asked.

"I do. And you have my Aunt Sophia's address? And Benni and Farah's?"

I did.

He gave me the Land Rover as a goodbye gift and taught me how to drive stick shift as we drove to Nairobi airport. We waited together quietly in plastic chairs, holding hands until his flight was called in English, crackling over the loudspeaker.

This was it.

"Anna, this is what I've decided. I will write to you on this same day every year and I will ask you if you love me enough to come to Rome," he said, hoisting a canvas duffle bag strap onto his shoulder.

"Write to me before then. There will never be anyone else who will call me *carina*," I said, with a wave of grief so strong that I moaned. "And no one who will tell me to have *coraggio*."

Matteo laughed at the truth of that.

There was one last embrace, one last kiss, a stab of doubt that left me shaking in his arms, and one last wave back to me as he boarded the rollaway staircase to the plane. I ran up the stairs to the open viewing deck on the terminal roof, found the Alitalia plane waiting for its turn on the runway, and watched it take off. I couldn't see Matteo, but, if he could see me from his seat, I wanted his last image of Africa to be of me, searching for a last sight of him.

I allowed myself a cry—just a small, selfish one—for the heartbroken, twenty-one-year-old girl who wondered if anyone else would ever love her again. Tearfully, I made my way through the crowds of people to the parking lot and to my next challenge—how to get myself back to Nairobi on my own in a Land Rover with a manual transmission and twelve gears.

# 20/ The Dream: Nairobi, Kenya

The Nairobi I discovered during the days after Matteo left was a city that lived up to every one of my expectations. When I thought of him, I was disconsolate. I cried at night but, each new day, I jumped into the Land Rover and explored Nairobi, feeling like an actress in a movie. I had to remind myself every evening—this was my life.

There was an orphaned-animal park not far from Benni and Farah's bungalow that I visited every morning, bringing with me a basket of bananas and peelings. The game warden, a friend of Benni's, allowed me special access to the youngest animals, bringing me behind the barriers and into their pens. The orphans had been brought to the park from all over Kenya, having lost their mothers to poachers or predators when they were too young to survive on their own. I was permitted to hand-feed, pet, and play with them. There was a new arrival, a baby elephant the warden had named Kiki, who, after my second visit with bananas, began to wait for me in the morning by the fence to her enclosure.

"Come stand next to her and scratch her hide," the warden coaxed. "She's a baby. She misses her mama and needs affection. Just watch your feet. Step back, but lean slightly forward." He demonstrated how not to get stepped on by an elephant.

Kiki was grieving. She forlornly followed after another infant elephant, a young zebra foal, and me, wanting to be cuddled and petted. She sobbed for her mother—an unmistakable sound, even if one has never heard an elephant cry. At other times, she was a trickster, using her trunk to steal bananas from the basket, play with my hair, deliberately tickle my neck and ears, and push me from behind when I was paying attention to another animal. She had absolutely no fear of me.

Tourists disgorged from hotel buses all morning long and took snapshots of us, assuming I was a park employee. With one or two baby monkeys on my shoulders, the zebra colt eating corncobs from my hand, and Kiki messing with my hair on the other side, I did seem to fit in quite nicely.

Standing in a bank queue in downtown Nairobi on my first afternoon, I stared at the other people in line—stereotypes from every book I'd ever read set in Africa and every African movie I'd ever seen. There was a white hunter/game-warden type in his khakis, knee-high socks, and pocketed vest, a rifle slung casually over his shoulder and a holstered pistol on his hip. Behind him, smoking a cigarette from a long filter between her pink manicured nails, was a beautiful white woman with long, brown hair, wearing knee-high, gleaming leather riding boots, ivory jodhpurs, and a long, trailing printed silk scarf wrapped around her neck. Behind her, a stoic Masai elder, tall and stringy and wrapped in red and white checked fabric, stood patiently waiting his turn. He stood balanced like a stork on one leg, leaning on his spear, wearing empty, black 35mm film canisters as earrings in the three-inch drooping holes in his earlobes.

As a houseguest of Benni and Farah's, who had made many friends quickly in the time they had lived in Nairobi, I was introduced to the luxurious world of the British expats.

They built English Tudor homes and grew English cottage gardens. They ate English and Indian food on silver platters served by white-gloved Kenyan servants. They built private boarding schools for their children that rivaled the best schools in England, and played English sports like cricket, rugby, polo, and football. They lived a lifestyle they would never have been able to afford in England—magnificent gardens, horses, polo matches, hunts, safaris, and country weekends on farms of thousands and thousands of acres. They behaved like eccentric British aristocracy— slightly mad, in a world of their own, and, in many ways, delusional.

Most remembered the Mau Mau Uprising in 1952—the machete and spear attacks on white farmers and their families by Kenyans north of Nairobi that had terrorized all the farmers and expats in East Africa. At that time, the desire for freedom from colonial rule was sweeping across Africa. The thirty thousand whites living in Kenya had ruled over the five million blacks since the end of the nineteenth century when England had declared Kenya a colony, confiscating the most fertile land for coffee farms, over- riding tribal law with the British justice system, building roads and laying railroad track through tribal territories without any concern for the people who had lived there for five thousand years.

When the Africans rose up in revolt during the Mau Mau attacks, and once the British understood the house of cards they had built for themselves in Kenya and how precarious their safety, they relinquished the country. After a transition period for both governments to adjust, independence was granted in 1964, and Jomo Kenyatta, a former Mau Mau leader, became Kenya's first president. Every former colonist and expat I met still shivered at the mention of the Mau Mau Uprising, and almost all of them thought the country had gone to "bloody hell" since independence.

The expats wistfully talked about England as a beacon of civilization, but, given a choice between the gray, damp sameness of England's modern cities and suburbs, and the raucous fecundity of Africa, they chose Africa. They grumbled into their shandies and sundowners about "the bloody Africans," but rushed back there with relief after their holidays back home, knowing they could never return to the dreary rain and the ordinariness of life in England.

When they spoke of "home," it was never Kenya, but rather an idealized vision of England. They still believed in the supremacy of the British Empire, but they loved Kenya, too, with all its complications. They remembered Kenya as a true Garden of Eden in the days before the Mau Mau, before independence.

Some people come into our lives by chance and, by their example or encouragement, they change everything. Benni and Farah were that for me. Matteo dropped me at their doorstep and left for Rome without knowing the great gift he was giving me. They took me in, a stranger from another country. In me, they recognized qualities in themselves. I was curious, adventurous, unformed, and loved Africa as they did. They opened themselves to me and turned every idea I had about work and love upside down.

Farah was a traditional homemaker—she home-schooled their ten-year-old son, David, cleaned the house, prepared all the family meals with only part time help, and hung piles of laundry to dry on clotheslines in the African sun. And yet, she was the most extraordinary woman. She assisted Benni, traveling to the most inhospitable places in the world with him when he needed an unpaid assistant, packing and unpacking his camera equipment, labeling and archiving his photographs, and offering her opinions on the images and on his future projects.

She was also an artist and, when there was any time for herself, she sculpted in metal and driftwood in her own studio, selling her work in galleries throughout East Africa and Scandinavia.

Unlike Signora Manfriando's mealtime extravaganzas, Farah cooked simple vegetarian food. At her table a pot of soup; a bowl of stewed beans, garlic, and herbs; and a platter of roasted sweet potato halves became a feast. She was all about plentiful, healthy, fast, and easy, and she taught me kitchen shortcuts that I use to this day. Unlike Matteo's mother, who would never think of serving day-old bread to her family as anything other than bread crumbs, Farah showed me how to sprinkle water on a loaf of dry bread, lightly rub the crust all over, and heat it in an oven until it smelled and tasted freshly baked. I learned from her example that a house needs four things to feel like a home—books, flowers, music, and the aroma of food cooking in the kitchen.

I recently found an old, grainy, black and white Christmas card photograph of them in swimsuits doing very advanced yoga poses on the front lawn of their bungalow. In the photo, Benni and Farah look exactly like what they were—vibrant, creative, adventurous. They were the first people I met who practiced yoga, lit incense, and chanted "Om." They walked around the house naked and unfazed by company, and they each took occasional lovers with not even a ripple of distress on the surface of their marriage. They shook up every single idea an American, middle-class girl like me had about relationships between men and women. I learned to relax a little, to judge less, and to accept there are many different ways to live life.

They were a young couple, living life completely on their own terms, creating a life and a family without any outside pressures or expectations. They were deeply committed to each other and yet sexually free in a way I had only read about in women's magazines. It was eye opening for me— the good daughter, the smart student, the girl in the front row of the class who always had the correct answer and her hand in the air, the compliant girlfriend who rarely made a sound during sex for fear of waking a sleeping brother.

I loved what I saw in Benni and Farah—two people who'd created lives uniquely suited to them. I wanted to be like Benni and build a career out of my curiosity and creativity. And I wanted to be like Farah—a generous, respected, intelligent partner, wife, and mother.

Benni was a nature photographer; a patient, obsessive, and original one whose images captured the common emotions humans and animals share. His extraordinary photographs of elephants helped to educate people around the world about the deep bonds between herd members. His wildebeest photographs introduced the world to their yearly four-thousand-mile migration across Africa.

While I was staying in Nairobi, his studio was filled with hundreds of photographs of chimpanzees, clipped to multiple wires strung across the room like clotheslines—the results of a four-month-long trip to the Uganda rain forest. He was analyzing and selecting the photos for an article in a science journal with a Swedish biologist who was writing the text. I was drawn to Benni's work, unable to keep away.

"How ever did you capture these shots?" I asked, amazed at the images strung around the room. The photographs were close-ups of chimpanzee youngsters playing with each other on a log, on low tree limbs, in the dirt, sharing food, pulling up roots. Benni had captured emotions in the faces of these young chimpanzees—affection, laughter, and jealousy.

"You walk uphill through the rain forest for miles and for hours and, when you find a chimpanzee troop, you stop and make yourself invisible and don't move. It takes days and days of sitting perfectly still, allowing the mosquitoes to swarm you and the insects to crawl up your arms and legs and bite you, before the chimpanzees allow you close enough to photograph them," Benni replied.

"You sit there, hungry and stiff all day, wanting to scratch a bite, unable to move a muscle or scream as you watch a snake slither across your leg. You want to take a sip of water, but you know you shouldn't risk making the smallest movement toward your canteen hanging only millimeters away at your side. You cover yourself and your camera equipment with a tarpaulin when it rains—which, in the rain forest, it does every day—and you sweat through your clothes in the steam of the afternoon. Oh, and I almost forgot," Benni added. "You can't move, so you piss through your shorts leg, right where you're crouching."

"It sounds wonderful," I sighed.

Benni laughed. "That's what Farah said to me when we first met and I described my work to her. It's why I married her."

"I'd love to take pictures like these," I said, waving my arms around the studio.

"Well, we're taking you out into the bush for a few days while you're here. I'll show you how the Nikons and the lenses work together, and we'll see how you shoot."

With those words, my life took a direction I never could have imagined. Once I held a camera in my hand, looked through the view finder, and, later, saw my first negatives and prints, I was hooked.

# 21/ Safari: The Kenya Bush and the Lamu Archipelago

We left for the bush a few days later—Benni; Farah; David; me; Stefan, the visiting biologist/writer from Sweden; and Peyter, a South African safari guide and yet another friend of Benni's. We took along Jamal, Farah's houseboy, as our cook and camp manager, and his young son as his helper and as a companion for David.

I loved every bit of safari life—the planning; the lists; the shopping for sugar, loose tea, corn meal, paraffin, and batteries; the packing against checklists; the jerry cans of water and petrol; and the battered Land Rovers covered in dried mud up to the sunshades. I loved the journey as a caravan; the bouncing for hours on the hard seats, nodding off from the sameness of the landscape and the heat of the afternoon; then setting up camp and unloading all the equipment we had brought with us—the canvas tents, the camp shower, camp beds, sleeping bags, the oil lamps, the tin pots and frying pans, the mosquito nets.

I loved the food—the milky, sweet hot tea in the still-dark mornings; the lunches of bread and cheese, sitting on top of the Land Rovers; the dinners of bean and vegetable stews and cornmeal porridge around the large fire that burned all night; and cold Kenyan beer after a hot day of game watching.

And, of course, there were the animals—moments of splendor, of the certainty of God's touch, and moments of horror and terror.

Our first evening in our campsite, I left the fire to grab my forgotten flashlight from my tent. Suddenly, I heard a lion roar right in my left ear. I smelled him—a rank, animal smell like a horse barn mixed with cat urine. He was out of sight in the dark, in the tall grasses bordering the ring of tents, but it sounded like he was right next to me. I ran to the nearest tent and dove onto a camp bed, shaking with fear. I heard everyone calling my name and I tried to yell for them, but, in my total panic, I wasn't capable of yelling very loudly.

It was young David, all by himself, who pushed through the tent flap, shining his flashlight in my face.

"What happened to you, Annie? Where have you been? There's a lion in the bushes. We heard it just now. We thought you were dragged off and eaten!"

To my ears, he sounded all too excited by the possibility.

"David, please, you stay right here with me," I answered, grabbing his arm and sitting him down by my side. I zipped the tent up, only an illusion of safety. "Let's yell together for your father and tell him we're okay." We screamed until Benni and Peyter unzipped it again.

They searched the perimeter of the camp with headlamps and rifles, but the lion had disappeared into the night. They thought I had exaggerated how close the lion had been to me, but I stuck to my story. I knew how loud it had been in my ear and how overpowering the odor.

That first night, the screeching, the hooting, the rustling, the snapping of branches, and the cries from the bush kept me awake. I lay in my sleeping bag, listening to roaring lions, howling hyenas, monkeys in the creaking tree limbs above us, and some kind of animal, snorting and stamping and brushing up against the sides of the tent. I was too afraid to look out into the dark to see what it was, but something was definitely out there.

In the morning, Peyter pointed out footprints on the ground and surmised that a herd of elephants had moved through our camp during the night. He told us the animals often wander through in the dark, unable to tell the difference between a canvas tent and a brick wall. They maneuver around the tents as they would around a tree or a rock.

The plan for one afternoon was a walk across a flat plain to a nearby river to watch hippos. All during lunch, Peyter scanned the dry, golden plains through his binoculars, looking for possible danger. He eventually felt confident we could start our walk safely. He carried a rifle across his chest and a pistol strapped to his calf and cautiously led us out into the low grass.

As we walked, we could see a few Cape buffalo grazing in the distance, nothing to worry about. They had been grazing all through our lunch and siesta, but, as we continued, we saw more and more of them along the horizon. Soon, Cape buffalo surrounded us on three sides and even Peyter, the only one of us with weapons, started to panic. When he told us, in a low and urgent voice, to walk to the nearest tree for cover as quickly as we could, I knew we really were in trouble. The trees he pointed to were no more than a foot in diameter, not big enough to protect us from a strong wind.

*This is really happening,* I thought. *This is no ride at Disneyland...I could be trampled by a herd of stampeding buffalo in the next few minutes.*

We had hired a local Masai tracker for the duration of the journey, wrapped in a red and white checked cloth hanging from beneath his armpits and an old red blanket tossed over his shoulders like a cape, a frail old man with arms and legs like twigs. He looked like he weighed no more than eighty pounds.

Along with his spear and hand-painted shield, he carried with him two whittled sticks about sixteen inches long and two inches in diameter, each with a knob on one end. He marched right up to the Cape buffalo he had decided was the leader of the herd and stopped perhaps twenty-five feet away. He banged the two sticks together in the buffalo's face. Nothing happened...a standoff. He went a little closer and banged the sticks together again. Nothing.

Then he moved right into the Cape buffalo's face. He was ten feet away from a twelve-hundred-pound wild animal with pointed horns and hooves. He banged the sticks one more time. This time, the leader thought twice about taking on the old Masai. With a last shake of his head and a fed-up snort, it veered off into denser bush and the rest of the herd followed.

The Masai stood tall and still for a few moments, every sense alert, spear planted in the ground, until the big, old Cape buffalo completely disappeared into the bush. Only then did he turn around and wave for us to come forward. Hearts pounding, we cautiously moved from behind our trees—including Peyter, our sheepish safari guide—and continued our trek in search of those hippos in the river.

That was one of many life lessons I learned in Africa—how to face my biggest fears. Throughout my life, whenever I find myself mentally surrounded by Cape buffalo, I stand right up to them and bang two sticks together.

Most of our days on safari were spent game watching from behind a camera lens. We'd wake while it was still dark in order to be dressed, breakfasted, and out in the Land Rovers as the sun came up. The wild animals woke hungry and ready to hunt for their breakfast, and we were there to capture it. Benni kept me by his side and taught me how to gauge the light and distance, to focus, to be patient with the setup, and ready for that explosive moment there was no way to prepare for.

When we returned to Nairobi, we spent hours in the dark room, developing black and white 35mm film and printing the negatives. We analyzed with magnifying glasses our color slide images on Benni's large light box, discussed which were the best images and why, then waited for our prints to come back from the color lab in downtown Nairobi. This was the old-fashioned way one practiced photography.

With a digital camera and Photoshop, it is so much easier to produce great technical images, but it still takes the photographer with an artistic vision and the patience to capture the moment. After that safari, I was never again without a camera, always happiest exploring and documenting the people inhabiting the wildest places left on earth.

"You're good enough," Benni pronounced. "You have a lifetime to learn. Keep going and be ready for those moments."

The next weekend, Farah and I took off for the beach. We flew to

Mombasa, with our final destination Lamu, a small archipelago in the Indian Ocean. As soon as I saw the Peponi Hotel, brilliantly white in the sun, I knew I had come to a special place. It was a small, isolated, family hotel, owned by a Swedish mother and son, located on a soft white sand beach with not another hotel in sight. Everything about it was simultaneously both modest and luxurious, from flowers from the garden displayed in a jelly jar to a feather quilt for my bed.

There were almost no guests at the hotel, and only a local fisherman or two sailed up, beached their wooden boats, and offered fish to the kitchen. We woke, drank café au lait, walked out to the beach, shook out our wraps on the white sand, and sunbathed nude. We floated in the gentle ocean, barely exerting the energy to swim, and bared our souls to each other for three days, cementing a friendship that has remained constant throughout most of our lives. At the Peponi, with Farah as a different kind of safari guide, I learned to appreciate the sensual—the sun, the breeze off the ocean, the hot sand, the warm saltwater, the cool bed sheets, all against my skin, not caring about the time, or the day, or who saw me naked.

A bomb exploded outside the American Embassy in Nairobi while we were in Lamu, with many people hurt, and, when we returned to the city, we found it still reeling. An Islamic group claimed responsibility for the attack. Benni and Farah knew people who had been injured and a few who had lost their lives. They became caught up in rounds of hospital visits, funerals, and condolence visits, with more important things to do than shepherd an American guest around.

As I wrote a postcard to my parents to tell them I was okay, I knew it was time to go home. Suddenly fearful, feeling the full weight of my escape from Mekele and the terrorist bombing of a building I had driven by tens of times during my stay in the city, I missed home, missed my family, and didn't want to worry them any longer. I was ready to go back to New York, anxious to make my new life happen.

I feared I'd lost my chance at love and wondered if I would ever have it again, but I knew I had gained so much in its place—a new sense of myself and a direction for a career, a way of life I loved. I had known it as a child with a child's wisdom and now, as a woman, I also knew it to be true. This part of the world, Africa, made me happy.

"Don't take Daisy back to New York City," Farah begged. "She's happy here with our dogs and she has space to run and play. You can't keep her cooped up in an apartment. She's an African dog now. We want to keep her here so you'll come back. Sooner or later, you will return."

It didn't seem fair to bring Daisy back to a life where she could only dream of Africa, of chasing hyenas and monkeys down the hill, dozing her life away on a living room couch.

"I'll be back," I promised, brushing away my tears as I stroked her, reluctant to let my sweet Daisy go, but knowing she loved her life there. "Let me come up with a plan."

I was torn—homesick for my family and already homesick for Africa. From the minute I boarded my flight home, I began to plot my return. From then on, I would always find my way back to Africa.

# Preview of Longing for Africa Part Two: Kenya

Manhattan was as different from Kenya as two places could possibly be.

The equatorial sunlight bathed the African plains, the farms, and the Nairobi office buildings with molten gold. The New York City sun was a rarity, glimpsed through the canyons of concrete when I looked up at the sky and remembered I was, indeed, outdoors.

Kenya was green and brown and golden—the fruit trees and coffee plants, the people, the animals. Manhattan was gray—the sky, the clouds, the office towers of reflecting glass, the sidewalks, and the streets.

Time stood still in Kenya. Life there was lived as it had been for five thousand years, and to the same rhythm. New Yorkers couldn't move fast enough, accompanied by a different beat—the rifle-fire staccato of shoe heels against lobby marble floors; of taxi horns and squealing, worn-out brakes; the bells of messenger boys on bikes weaving through the city streets; and the start and stop of pedestrian traffic, moving in concert with the green and red traffic lights on every corner.

New York had its own beauty, a powerful energy carried on a song just barely beyond the range of human hearing. It whispered a promise of a brilliant future. Kenya offered the music and timelessness of nature; the stored memories of the earliest man. It whispered a promise, too: life would endure. I was excited by New York, but it was Kenya I loved.

When I first returned to New York, I moved to Greenwich Village and a fifth-floor, walk-up, corner apartment with two bedrooms, a bathtub in the kitchen, and a pizza parlor on the ground floor. The windows looked out on Bleecker and MacDougal Streets—the heart of the Village. I loved the apartment, but, when my mother saw it for the first time, she was horrified. "I've spent my whole life trying to get away from this neighborhood, this kind of life," she cried.

The skills I had developed in Africa were of little use in Manhattan. I could see across mountains, but I had difficulty climbing and descending subway stairs without holding tight to the metal banisters. In the year I had been in Ethiopia, I'd forgotten how to balance to carry out such a simple task. My sense of smell was keener, but the streets and alleys of Manhattan overflowed with garbage, and, rather than the aroma of Africa I had grown to love, New York simply stank. New Yorkers ignored the stench as well as they could as they hurried past.

151

Manhattan women were stylishly dressed in slight variations of city fashion—an all-black, narrow silhouette accessorized with black ballerina flats or high heels, and an expensive handbag. I clung to my khakis, my climbing boots, and canvas camera bag. I longed for East Africa every day and refused to give up the girl I had been to squeeze myself into the New York fashion scene. Sometimes I earned a raised eyebrow, or I sensed the ghost of a question on someone's lips, but, more often, I was dismissed with a sneer. I was no longer a New York girl. I didn't fit, didn't care, and never would again.

My first job when I returned was as a sketch artist and photographer for a syndicated newspaper columnist, magazine writer, and editor. It was a job that would help me to decompress and ease back into the hellish pace of the garment industry.

Deidre wrote about fashion trends and trendsetters. She had moved to Manhattan from Southern California to be at the center of the publishing business. She was Helen Gurley Brown's perfect *Cosmopolitan* woman, in charge of her career and her love life. "Having it all" was a catchphrase at that time, coined by Helen Gurley Brown, and, to me, Deidre was its poster child—a sculptor, live-in boyfriend; a great East Side apartment; published books; a newspaper column; and free-lance magazine assignments. She was living the city life most *Cosmopolitan*-reading women of that time dreamed about.

Even in the late seventies, at the end of the hippie movement and right in the middle of women's fight for birth control, abortion rights, and equality in the workplace, most women still saw marriage as the brass ring. I wanted love, marriage, and babies too, but, after my life in Africa, I wanted more than that.

Ten years older than me, Deidre became a role model and another lifelong friend, showing me the way.

"What about love and marriage and children?" I asked her. There was a part of me still my mother's daughter, but I wasn't ready to turn in my climbing boots for a ruffled hostess apron just yet.

"Don't worry about that," she promised. "Work. Follow what you're curious about, and love will find you."

My job was to provide the accompanying images for Deidre's weekly articles. I rushed all over Manhattan with my camera bag over my shoulder, sketchpad under one arm, and a tripod under the other. I met Deidre in front of stately apartments and mansions on the Upper East Side, in garment district sample rooms and showrooms, and loft buildings on the streets of Chinatown, Little Italy, and Soho, ready to interview people like Diane Von Furstenburg, Calvin Klein, Ralph Lauren, Betsey Johnson, and Andy Warhol.

Deidre warned me to stay quiet during these interviews and to take my cues from her. I learned a great deal by watching from the sidelines, silently sketching or setting up the lighting for the photo shoots, and I listened intently as these people opened up to Deidre.

These famous, creative individuals were no different from anyone else. They came from regular families, big cities or small towns, public or private schools. They were college graduates and high school dropouts. Some were naturally good-looking and others needed relentless grooming and heavy makeup.

They had cut from the herd when they discovered their talents and their passions were aligned. They had believed in themselves and had worked hard to accomplish what they had dreamed of as teenagers, pushing their goals out farther and farther as they achieved success way beyond their original goals. In that way, they were different. But they also were quite normal. They had messy hair, bad breath, or acne on their jaw line. Their stomachs growled. They could be sloppy or meticulous, preoccupied or gracious, bitchy or kind, just like the rest of us. Except for their talent and focus, they were ordinary.

This new understanding gave me the courage to begin a book of my own, a series of interviews and photographs with modern day explorers. I chose some of the world's most well-known adventurers—revered mountain climbers, wildlife experts, river and ocean explorers. I was curious about them and wanted to know why they had chosen their solitary and contrary paths, and how they had fought the pressures of family and modern life to become who they were. These were my own struggles, and I wanted to learn how other people found their way through them.

Deidre had taught me that celebrities were more accessible than I might imagine. She simply dialed the number and asked for an interview, and usually the response would be enthusiastic. Even without credentials, the explorers I'd chosen readily agreed to my requests. Not one of them turned me down. I only had to get myself to where they were. I saved every penny I could and bought airline tickets to places as near as Philadelphia, or as far away as India.

The title of my book, *Because I Couldn't Dance*, came from the answer a mountain climber gave to my question about his early influences. His mother had given him an Outward Bound course that began the day before his senior prom. He told me she had arranged the timing because she knew he couldn't dance. *Ahhh*, I thought, recognizing myself—*awkward, out of sync, born into a supportive family, but belonging elsewhere.*

As I observed those New York fashion icons from behind my camera lens and as I interviewed those amazing explorers, my longing for Africa and adventures of my own became overwhelming. I, too, wanted to live my life as bravely as they did.

In the meantime, a fashion design job interview took me to Los

Angeles. It was for a position designing girls' sportswear for a company whose clothing I had seen, loved, and followed in Bloomingdale's. I had called and asked if they needed a designer and they had called back.

"No one has ever approached us like this before," the owner said. "Come to Los Angeles and let's meet. We're small, but we're growing, and maybe the time is right to hire a designer."

I eventually met him at a gas station in the San Fernando Valley. The engine warning light had come on in my rental car as I made my way across the unfamiliar city. Exiting across six lanes of ferocious L.A. freeway traffic, I pulled into a gas station to call him.

"Where are you?" he asked.

I had no idea, but asked a man walking past me at the pumps. I parroted back into the phone what I was told.

"Wait right there. You're not far," the owner said. "I'm on my way."

A half hour later, a man pulled up in a bright red Mercedes convertible and grinned up from the driver's seat. I knew, even before I saw his warehouse and the sample room, before I met his wife and my future patternmaker and sample makers, that this job would be right for me and that I already loved this city filled with sunlight, the craziest traffic, and red Mercedes convertibles.

He hired me because he liked me—hardly because my résumé was stellar. It was a serendipitous move for me, joining this girls' jeans and sportswear company on its way to household name status. It carried me along in its wake to tremendous success, to my first home, and a Southern California beach life. Creatively, I blossomed.

My house was the smallest on one of Malibu's nicest beaches, with a famous *Sports Illustrated* swimsuit model as a neighbor on one side and a genuine Beatle on the other. Movie and TV stars, musicians, singers, and directors strolled along the beach beyond my deck, waving to be friendly as we passed each other on the beach. When I grocery shopped, or picked up a pizza or a magazine, I never knew who I would see. That was always fun, but the only celebrity who ever turned me into a speechless, gaping fool was Elizabeth Taylor passing me in a food aisle, pushing a grocery cart.

I traveled a great deal for work, racing through the world's airports and looking the part of an eccentric fashion designer. I never gave up my safari wardrobe, drove a mud-splattered Jeep that was rarely washed, and my camera bag always traveled with me.

I was happy with my life and my good fortune. I wished I had a boyfriend, someone who would last for more than two or three dates, but I longed for East Africa even more. I wanted so much to go back and I thought long and hard about how I could return there in a more meaningful way than a ten-day vacation safari.

My childhood Africa scrapbook had been lost, either in the move from my parents' home to my Greenwich Village apartment, in my parents' move from New York to Florida, or in my cross-country move to California. I had replaced it with my own memories, a few precious photographs, phone calls to Gemma—now divorced from "Dean, darling"—and letters back and forth to Benni and Farah in Nairobi.

Once a month, I wrote to Amira and helped her with her studies. I heard nothing from Matteo and found myself unable to complete a letter of my own to him. I assumed he had found someone new and had moved on, perhaps had even married. I pictured him that way, beside a pretty, pregnant wife with long, dark hair.

My daydreams were of Africa, and at night I dreamed of her, too—of the wildlife grazing on the plains; of Lela in her brilliant saris and musical bracelets; of Amira, Daisy, and Negiste; of Matteo and the Manfriandos; the tribes we had met on our road trip safari out of Ethiopia; and of the dazed and weakened faces of children in the Mekele refugee camp.

I woke from these dreams longing for Africa.

An idea for a new book began to form. I would write and photograph a series of children's books on how children lived in different parts of the world. I loved adventure travel, photography, writing, and children. I'd combine all those interests in this series, once a year choosing a new country to write about. I'd live with the tribes and photograph the kids, document their everyday lives, and then come back and share it with American children. Ever since coming home from Ethiopia and Kenya, I'd wanted to share what I'd learned in Africa—that we're all the same beneath our clothing and decorations, wherever we're from, whatever our customs.

Writing and photographing one book a year would allow me to explore the remote and wild places left on earth and still keep on working as a clothing designer during the rest of the year. I wanted to visit New Guinea, Indonesia, rural China, the Amazon, and Thailand, but Kenya would be the first in the series. It would finally take me back to Africa with a purpose.

I would see Benni and Farah and Daisy again. And, in a country I loved and was familiar with, I could discover if I had the stamina and physical ability to live among the world's most primordial people.

I planned a trip that would allow me to live for three weeks at a time with three different tribes that fascinated me, indigenous people who lived as they had for thousands of years. Hopefully, they would trust me enough to accept and include me in their day-to-day lives and celebrations.

I chose the Samburu tribe who wandered their ancestral lands with their livestock and whose entire world was built around their cattle, camels, and goats. I added the Turkanas for a complete contrast—fishermen who lived along Lake Turkana, in one of the hottest, driest, and most inhospitable places on earth. After the tribes, I would finish with the Swahilis—Islamic craftsmen and artisans who had settled in the cities and villages along the Indian Ocean. And, when I was done with the camping, the photographing, and the research, I'd treat myself and go back to my favorite hotel in my favorite place in the whole world one more time—the Peponi Hotel on Lamu Island.

I'd been aching to return to the Peponi since I had gone there with Farah three years before. I often daydreamed about sleeping once again in the hotel's white-painted beds with their ironed, light blue and white striped sheets, eating fresh fish under a ceiling of intertwining boughs of bougainvillea, and swimming in the warm Indian Ocean.

Camping beside the two tribes inland, retreating to the ocean and the Peponi Hotel to recover and use it for a staging area for my forays into the city to photograph the Swahili children, that was my idea of a perfect trip.

I pitched the book series to a major publisher the next time I was in New York for business. I simply called the children's book editor, as Deidre would have done, and asked for an appointment. To my astonishment, I got it, showed my photographs, and discussed ideas for the series. I was excited to be given the go-ahead for the first book on Kenya, a contract to sign, and an advance that would finance the trip. It was my first pitch to an editor, and I had no idea how lucky I was to walk away with a book deal, maybe even a multi-book deal.

My boss generously agreed to an extended vacation. I'd be gone from work for two months—a lot of time for a fashion designer—missing two monthly collections.

"You go, Annie," he said. "You do this. You're young. You're talented. Go. We'll be here when you get back."

I was finally on my way back to Africa. I had all the confidence in the world that everything would work out...

# Contact the Author

I sincerely thank you for reading this book and hope you enjoyed it. I would be extremely grateful if you could leave a review on Amazon.

I'd love to hear your comments and am happy to answer any questions you may have. There are also many photographs of my time in Africa on my website. Do please get in touch with me by:

Email: annieschrank@yahoo.com

Facebook: facebook.com/annie.schrank

Website: www.annieschrank.com

Twitter: @annieschrank1

LinkedIn: www.linkedin.com/in/annie-schrank-5575379b

To receive notification of my next book, please join my mailing list now: www.eepurl.com/cSw39P

If you enjoy memoirs, I recommend you pop over to Facebook group We Love Memoirs to chat with me and other authors there. www.facebook.com/groups/welovememoirs

I look forward to hearing from you.


Annie Schrank

# Acknowledgments

This book has been seven years in the making, and I had the help and support of so many people along the way.

Thank you to my online writers' group filled with talented, generous people I adore but have never met in person including Peter Pekin in Chicago and Cindy Dwyer in Connecticut. I was fortunate enough to meet Peggy Vincent in her home in Berkley, California. She believed in my writing ability and my manuscript from the first moment I joined the group. Without her, there would be no book, I'm quite sure.

The group taught me how to really write a memoir and insisted I go deeper, and then deeper still. We've shared six years of hard work together, turning a sketch of an idea by a stranger who'd only written magazine articles into a memoir that can make people cry.

Thanks to my agent, Felicia Eth, for believing in my manuscript and working so hard to sell it, and to Jacky Donovan from Ant Press for her insightful editing and patience.

From Disney World, I'd like to thank Jackie Ogden and Dr. Beth Stevens. They read my manuscript, loved it, and passed it to Dr. Jane Goodall, my idol, to read and offer a review. (And huge thanks to Dr. Goodall for agreeing.)

Thank you to my Disney colleagues for their creative help—to Josh Deckard for the clean design of my website, book jacket, and his photography, all of which capture the real me; and to Amanda Metri for the map of Ethiopia that does so much to anchor this memoir to its place in the world.

I'm grateful to my women's book club members—Carrie Stewart, Claudia Schoener, Maria Londono, Karen Cala, Marita Sonnerborg, Donna Hill, and Erja Julius—who read an early manuscript and sat for seven hours in my home discussing it and loving it. They made me believe for the first time that maybe I did have a story to tell that could move people to tears. A story good enough to share with the world.

Thank you to my mother, Daisy, and my father, Howard, both gone now, for allowing me to discover who I was, even if it would never be a suburban Cinderella. And thank you to my daughter, Darlene, and to her daughter, Ava. I wrote this book for them, so they can really know what their mother and grandmother was like in her youth.

Thank you once again to my Grover for having my back always and surrounding me with so much love and care.

Thank you all. I'm truly grateful when I think of the wonderful people in my life.

# Ant Press Books

If you enjoyed this book, you may also enjoy these titles:

## MEMOIR

*Chickens, Mules and Two Old Fools* by Victoria Twead
(Wall Street Journal Top 10 bestseller)
*Two Old Fools ~ Olé!* by Victoria Twead
*Two Old Fools on a Camel* by Victoria Twead
(New York Times bestseller x 3)
*Two Old Fools in Spain Again* by Victoria Twead
*One Young Fool in Dorset* by Victoria Twead
*One Young Fool in South Africa (The Prequel)* by Joe and Victoria Twead

*Heartprints of Africa: A Family's Story of Faith, Love, Adventure, and Turmoil* by Cinda Adams Brooks

*Into Africa with 3 Kids, 13 Crates and a Husband* by Ann Patras
*More into Africa: 3 Kids, Some Dogs and a Husband* by Ann Patras

*Simon Ships Out: How One Brave, Stray Cat Became a Worldwide Hero* by Jacky Donovan
*Smoky: How a Tiny Yorkshire Terrier Became a World War II American Army Hero, Therapy Dog and Hollywood Star* by Jacky Donovan
*Smart as a Whip: A Madcap Journey of Laughter, Love, Disasters and Triumphs* by Jacky Donovan

*Fat Dogs and French Estates ~ Part I* by Beth Haslam
*Fat Dogs and French Estates ~ Part II* by Beth Haslam
*Fat Dogs and French Estates ~Part III* by Beth Haslam

*How not to be a Soldier: My Antics in the British Army* by Lorna McCann

*Cane Confessions: The Lighter Side to Mobility* by Amy Bovaird

*Midwife: A Calling* by Peggy Vincent
*Midwife: A Journey* by Peggy Vincent

*Serving is a Pilgrimage* by John S. Basham

*Moment of Surrender: My Journey through Prescription Drug Addiction to Hope and Renewal* by Pj Laube

*One of its Legs are Both the Same* by Mike Cavanagh

*Horizon Fever* by A E Filby

## NON-FICTION

*How to Write a Bestselling Memoir* by Victoria Twead

## FICTION

*Parched* by Andrew C Branham

*A is for Abigail* by Victoria Twead (Sixpenny Cross 1)
*B is for Bella* by Victoria Twead (Sixpenny Cross 2)

## CHILDREN'S BOOKS

*Seacat Simon: The Little Cat Who Became a Big Hero* (age 8 to 11) by Jacky Donovan

*The Rise of Agnil* by Susan Navas (Agnil's World 1)
*Agnil and the Wizard's Orb* by Susan Navas (Agnil's World 2)
*Agnil and the Tree Spirits* by Susan Navas (Agnil's World 3)
*Agnil and the Centaur's Secret* by Susan Navas (Agnil's World 4)

*Morgan and the Martians* by Victoria Twead

Made in the USA
Middletown, DE
13 September 2018